FINDING YOUR

AFRICAN
AMERICAN ANCESTORS

A BEGINNER'S GUIDE

FINDING YOUR

AFRICAN
AMERICAN ANCESTORS

A BEGINNER'S GUIDE

David T. Thackery

Ancestry

Library of Congress Cataloging-in-Publication Data

Thackery, David T.
  Finding your African American ancestors : a beginner's guide / by
David T. Thackery.
      p. cm.
  Includes bibliographical references.
  ISBN 0-916489-90-6 (alk. paper)
  1. Afro-Americans—Genealogy—Handbooks, manuals, etc. 2.
Afro-Americans—Genealogy—Archival resources—Directories. I. Title.
  E185.96 .T425 2000
  929'.1'08996073—dc21
                                                00-011432

Published by Ancestry® Publishing, an
imprint of MyFamily.com, Inc.

P.O. Box 990
Orem, Utah 84059
www.ancestry.com

Cover image: Ellis Wilson, Funeral Procession, ca. 1940.
Courtesy of The Amistad Research Center
at Tulane University, New Orleans, Louisiana.

Several additional images were graciously contributed by Sunny Nash.

First Printing 2000
10 9 8 7 6 5 4 3 2 1

Printed in the United States of America

*"In all of us there is
a hunger, marrow deep,
to know our heritage—
to know who we are and
where we have come from."*

—*Alex Haley*

CONTENTS

ILLUSTRATIONS

FOREWORD

As curator of Local and Family History at the Newberry Library in Chicago for fifteen years, David Thackery was at the forefront of African American genealogy. In his own quiet way he made major contributions to the field, delivering an occasional lecture, writing articles for periodicals and chapters for books, peer reviewing articles by others, and developing one of the premiere library collections of African American genealogical resources.

David's lectures and writings evolved from studying African American genealogy and assisting individual genealogists. This experience proved to be a training ground to develop the expertise needed to create the Newberry Library's impressive African American collection. It was one of the first serious collections of African American genealogy in the country. He took great pride in developing the collection.

Between 1987 and 1990, he, along with others at Newberry Library, obtained over $60,000 in foundation grants that enabled Newberry to purchase books, periodicals, and microfilm records specifically for African American genealogy.

As part of the grant, David hired, trained, and assisted Dr. Deloris Palmer Woodtor in conducting community outreach in African American genealogy. He also co-authored *Case Studies in African American Genealogy* with Woodtor. It is a useful guide for beginning researchers. Woodtor went on to write *Finding A Place Called Home* published by Random House in 1999.

After acquiring the collection, David compiled and edited *Afro-American Family History at the Newberry Library: A Research Guide and Bibliography* in 1988. It set the standard for African American genealogy collection bibliographies in the country. It was updated in 1993 and he continually updated it, even providing unpublished updates for my genealogy classes twice a year.

When called upon to write the African American genealogy chapter in the revised edition of *The Source: A Guidebook of American Genealogy*, David was uniquely qualified for the job. His essays are thoughtful, insightful, and illustrate his study and understanding of sources for African American genealogy. The text he prepared for that publication makes up a portion of this book. Though it was written before the genealogy boom on the Internet, David's coverage of sources for African American genealogy in the pages that follow is very relevant. Researchers must understand the traditional sources that David included in this book to put information located on the Internet in perspective.

The field of African American genealogy is in need of good texts and David knows quality when he sees it. I recall many conversations with him on quality control in library acquisitions. It is from him I learned that several genealogical authors omitted African Americans from their transcriptions and indexes. He took a firm stand and refused to continue to purchase these works for Newberry's collection. On a similar vein, he also refused to place on the shelf works by African American authors that did not live up to basic genealogical standards.

Both of these courageous acts of quality control have helped researchers studying African American genealogy. Works of the first part lead researchers astray, thinking their ancestors were not in given areas because they were omitted from the book. Works from the second category divert novice researchers from following sound genealogical techniques.

David's untimely death in 1998 at the age of forty-five was a great loss to Newberry Library, the genealogical community, and to me personally. David was a fellow colleague, a fellow member of the Board of Friends of Genealogy at Newberry Library, a dear friend, and a rare individual. His contributions will be hard to duplicate.

David will surely be missed as his efforts are appreciated by the African American genealogy community. One of the reasons for the strong African American genealogical community in Chicago is due to the efforts of David Thackery's work at Newberry Library. This book will serve as a lasting legacy to his work, study, and unselfish attitude.

—Tony Burroughs
author of *Black Roots*

FINDING YOUR
AFRICAN AMERICAN
ANCESTORS

Few areas of American genealogy pose as much challenge as the search for African American ancestry prior to the Civil War. Notwithstanding the inherent difficulties, there are few areas that contain as much unrealized potential. Despite great strides within the last two decades, the basic outlines of the field are only now being clarified. While the difficulties of African American genealogical research are not to be discounted, these difficulties are not always insurmountable. As time goes on, the publication and indexing of pertinent genealogical source material may make success more often the rule than the exception. It is also to be hoped that, as more African Americans publish their findings, their research will contribute to the success of others, thus eventually forming a body of mutually supporting secondary literature. What helps one will ultimately help all.

Generally speaking, many of the basic tools of American genealogical research can be successfully applied to the investigation of an African American lineage going back to the Civil War. These include vital records, federal censuses, cemetery records, inscriptions, etc. Researchers should be aware, however, that many marriage, birth, and death records in the old slave states were, until recently, maintained in separate ledgers by local governments. The publication of vital records by local genealogical societies sometimes reflects this division. With the publication of indexes to the 1870 federal census enumerations, especially those for Southern states, it has become increasingly feasible for researchers of African American genealogy to trace a given line to that very important year in which ex-slaves were first enumerated as free people.

FREE BLACKS

At least one out of ten African Americans was already free when the first shots were fired on Fort Sumter. They were a diverse group. As with those who were enslaved, free African Americans could have racially mixed backgrounds encompassing African, Caucasian, and American Indian ancestry. Many of them came from families that had been free for several generations, perhaps stemming from the manumission of an ancestor or a liaison between an indentured white woman and a slave. Others were runaways who lived uncertain existences in the Northern states. Although not usually thought of in the category of "free black," one group enjoyed an essentially free status in affiliation with the Seminole Indians, while others formed elites in Charleston and Louisiana, where many were themselves slaveowners. They were farmers, servants, artisans, and sailors in the Northeast, in many instances descended from the slave populations that existed there when slavery was found above the Mason-Dixon line. (In the state of New York, for example, slavery was not completely abolished until 1827. Approximately ten thousand enslaved blacks were enumerated there in the 1820 census.) In parts of Ohio and Indiana, their presence was due largely to the efforts of North Carolina Quakers who manumitted their slaves and settled them in those areas. In the Border states, especially in Maryland, they made up a substantial proportion of the total black population, while in much of the Deep South they were only a tiny minority who occupied a precarious position at best.

Figure 1 - The wedding portrait of George and Rose Wilson who married at the end of the Civil War. George was a former slave from La Grange, Texas. Rose was from a free land owning family in Northern Brazos County in Texas. This picture was taken about 1866. Courtesy, Sunny Nash.

African American researchers must be open to the possibility of encountering an antebellum free black ancestor; at the same time, however, they should not expect to find one in a time or place where the free black population was small. For example, the chances would be much higher for having such an ancestor in Virginia than in Mississippi. As with any genealogical research, knowledge of the historical context is critical to success.

In many instances, the records that are of genealogical value in the study of antebellum free blacks will not differ substantially from the records of whites. For example, the census enumerated all free people, black or white, on the same schedules. On the other hand, the United States was a house divided. In many states free blacks were required to register proof of their status with the county government. Such documentation could take the form of copies of manumission papers or affidavits attesting birth to a free woman. Without such proof, free blacks risked abduction and enslavement, even in the North. These registers were also common in the upper South and Border states, where they not only provided protection for free blacks but also helped to prevent slaves from passing as free people. The free black registers of Virginia counties have been increasingly finding their way into print.[1] In one such register is the following noteworthy example:

> *I William Moss Clerk of the County Court of Fairfax do hereby certify that the bearer hereof Levi Richardson a light coloured black boy about twenty one years of Age five feet seven Inches high, large nose thin visage . . . a scar on the left side of his head is the son of Sally Richardson a free woman emancipated by Genl. George Washington deceased as appears by an Original Register heretofore granted by the County Court of Fairfax and this day surrendered. Whereupon at the request of the said Levi Richardson I have caused him to be Registered in my office according to law. Given under my hand this 19th day of November 1834.[2]*

Similar documentation can also be found in the courthouses of many Midwestern counties. For example, Wright State University microfilmed such records for the counties of Greene, Logan, Miami, and Montgomery in Ohio.[3] More were transcribed by Joan Turpin in *Register of Black, Mulatto and Poor Persons in Four Ohio Counties 1791-1861* (Bowie, Md.: Heritage Books, 1985). If such records, whether in the South, Midwest, or Northeast, are indeed extant, they are not likely to be among the easier documents to locate in the county courthouse. However, more are likely to surface with the passage of time, and they will perhaps be indexed and published as well. Many have also been microfilmed by the Genealogical Society of Utah.

---

1. see END NOTES on page 33

UNDERGROUND RAILROAD

From 1786 on, fugitive slaves could escape northward on the Underground Railroad, which covered fourteen northern states by 1830. From 1840 to 1860, some 50,000 slaves travelled it to settle in the North or in Canada (figure 2). The Federal Fugitive Slave Law of 1793 was countered by the Personal Liberty Laws of many northern states.

More than 15,000 free African Americans returned to Africa between 1821 and 1860. The colony of Liberia was established by the American Colonization Society in 1822 and became independent in 1847.

Figure 2 - Northern Routes of The Underground Railroad, 1840-60

THE TRANSITION FROM SLAVERY TO FREEDOM

At the time of the Civil War, the vast majority of African Americans were, of course, slaves. As such, they had no legal rights and could not even claim a legally recognized state of matrimony. Although records generated after emancipation can be very revealing, genealogically useful records documenting slave families which were contemporary to slavery are usually records, both private and public, concerned primarily with their owners. The researcher of slave genealogy therefore must know the identity of a slave's owner in order to research the slave. Slaveowning families—their migrations, births, deaths, and marital alliances—must therefore be the focus of research before any success can be achieved in tracing the lives of their slaves.

The search for the last slaveowner prior to emancipation then becomes the most important task. A common supposition is that emancipated slaves assumed the surnames of their last owners. If this had been the case in all instances, this critical stage of slave genealogy would be a less difficult one than it generally is; however, the truth is more complex, making research more problematic. Although there were many instances when the common assumption held true, there is ample evidence for slaves maintaining their own surname traditions, regardless of who their owners might have been.[4] Following emancipation, a slave did not necessarily assume a surname, but instead may have taken a name that had been in his or her family for several generations. A different surname than that of the last owner could, for example, be that of the owner of a grandparent, so such a name might be a valuable clue for future research.

More studies are still needed, but it is possible that there were regional patterns in this regard. For example, a study of a West Virginia county found no instances of ex-slaves with the surnames of their final owners,[5] while studies of Texas and South Carolina freed people indicate approximately a quarter to one third had the surnames of their last owners.[6] The signature book: f the Freedman's Savings and Trust (discussed in greater detail later) also provide evidence of the often confusing and unpredictable reality behind the surnames of ex-slaves. For example, one record from the Vicksburg, Mississippi branch names the parents of one Jesse Taylor as Robert and Nancy Page. A brother is listed as Simpson Roberts.[7] The complex nature of the "surname problem" should be kept in mind as the sources for African American genealogy are considered.

The Federal Censuses

It has already been noted that African Americans were enumerated as all other U.S. residents from 1870 (the first census year following the Civil War and emancipation) onward. Prior to 1870, however, the situation was far different. Although free African Americans were enumerated by name in 1850 and 1860, slaves were consigned to special, far less informative, schedules in which they were listed anonymously under the names of their owners. The only personal information provided was usually that of age, gender, and racial identity (either black or mulatto). As in the free schedules, there was a column in which certain physical or mental infirmities could be noted. In some instances the census takers noted an occupation, usually carpenter or blacksmith, in this column. Slaves aged 100 years or more were given special treatment; their names were noted, and sometimes a short biographical sketch was included. In at least one instance, that of 1860 Hampshire County, Virginia, the names of all slaves were included on the schedules, but this happy exception may be the only instance when the instructions were not followed.

Sometimes the listings for large slaveholdings appear to take the form of family groupings, but in most cases slaves are listed from eldest to youngest with no apparent effort to portray family structure. In any event, the slave schedules themselves almost never provide conclusive evidence for the presence of a specific slave in the household or plantation of a particular slaveowner. At best, a census slave schedule can provide supporting evidence for a hypothesis derived from other sources.[8] Prior to 1850 there were no special slave schedules for the manuscript census, as slave data was recorded as part of the general population schedules. In these, only the heads of household were enumerated by name.

In the absence of any contradictory information, it might be assumed that a family of freed people enumerated in the 1870 census was living not far from its last owner, whose surname they also bore. There would, of course, be reasons to dispute both assumptions. (Knowledge of the Civil War history of a locality could come into play here; for example, such relative stability would not have existed in a Georgia county that was in the path of Sherman's march to the sea.) Even so, this assumption represents one of the more obvious exploratory lines of research, especially in the absence of any other options. The first step in testing the hypothesis would

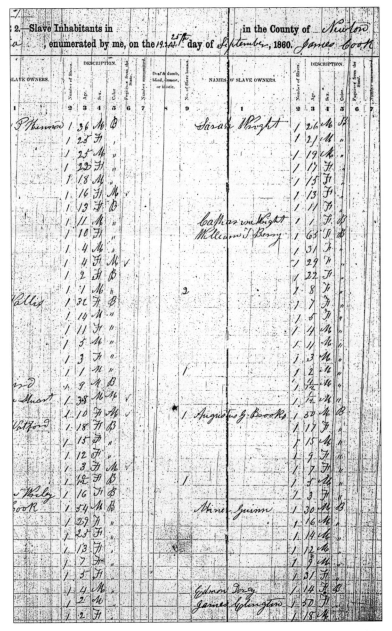

Figure 3 - A slave schedule from the 1860 Census for Newton County, Georgia, listing the name of the slave owner, number of slaves, and each slave's age, sex, and color.

Figure 4 - Detail of a financial and legal ledger from the Thomas S. Bocock Plantation in Appomattox Virginia. Shown is the total profit made from sales of slaves after the dissolution of the Bocock Estate. Courtesy of the University of Virginia Special Collections.

Mar	NOT NAMED	F	Malvina Hinkle	Pulaski	Cold	2 Mo
Jun	NOT NAMED (S)	F	James Hoge	"	Unknown	3 Da
7-11	SARAH J. HARROLD	F	H. & S. Harrold	"	Scarlet Fever	3-10
9-17	CHARLOTTE E. HUGE	F	J. & C. Trollinger	"	Unknown	23
12-25	MARY (S)	F	William Hoge	"	Pneumonia	20
Oct	LUCINDA HILL	F	A. & S. Odell	"	Consumption	35
Aug	JOHN H. HILL	M	H. H. Hill	"	Diarria	11
Feb	PETER (S)	M	James H. Hoge	"	Old Age	70
12-22	JAMES S. HOWARD	M	J.D. & A. Howard	"	Dropsey of Heart	13-01-10
4-15	JAMES H. HOLMES	M	"	"	"	1-02
Mar	HARRISON (S)	M	Joseph Graham	"	"	4
Feb	HARRIET (S)	F	Harvey Shepherd	"	Scarlet Fever	
Oct	NOT NAMED (S)	F	Elisabeth Kent	"	Not Known	18
8-8	MARY F. LITTLE	F	S. & A. Little	"	Scarlet Fever	3-01-25
8-11	WALTER C. LITTLE	M	"	"	"	6-15
Oct	NOT NAMED (S)	F	F.A. Morgan	"	Unknown	6
Oct	NOT NAMED (S)	F	"	"	"	3
4-9	SARAH E. MARTIN	F	W. & M. Martin	"	"	3
2-22	WILLIAM MARTIN	M	G. & M. Martin	"	Old Age	84
12-31	DOLLY ODEL	F	R. & S. Day	"	Unknown	35-06
12-23	RICHARD (S)	M	James H. Pierce	"	Smothered	5
Jan	BALLARD QUESENBERRY	M	Crockett E. Quesenberry	"	Fever	5
Feb	MARINDA QUESENBERRY	F	"	"	"	8
12-7	JOHN SUTTON	M	Unknown	"	"	64
Mar	ALEX (S)	M	H. Shepherd	"	"	10
6-24	THOMAS THORTON	M	"	"	Cholic	54-06
	REBECCA THORTON	F	"	"	Old Age	70
Aug	ELIZABETH VICKERS	F	H. & S. Vickers	"	Scarlet Fever	1-06
6-20	JOHN W. WALLACE	M	C. & N. Wallace	"	Unknown	20-11
10-1	FRANCIS (S)	F	Edwin Watson	"	Worms	5
Sep	PANTINA (S)	F	John Wygal	"	Unknown	2
Dec	GEORGE W. (S)	M	"	"	Cold	1-06
2-3	NOT NAMED	F	J. & M.S. Wygal	"	Infant Cholery	5

Figure 5 - A portion of a slavery record found in Births and Deaths 1853-1871 on Record in Pulaski County Court House, Pulaski Virginia (n.p., n.d.).

be to search for slaveowners of the same surname in the 1860 slave schedules of the county in which the African American family resided in 1870.
Starting in 1850, another supplemental schedule, the mortality schedule,
listed all deaths within a year before the regular census enumeration.[9] The
deaths of blacks and mulattoes, both free and slave, are recorded in them,
even though their names have not been included in many of the indexes to
these schedules.[10] The deaths of slaves were generally enumerated in four
fashions: unnamed (as in the slave schedules), but perhaps with the owner
identified; by first name only; by first name and surname; and by first
name with the owner noted.

Probate Records

Slaves were property. As distasteful as we find it today, this unfortunate
fact is the all-encompassing reality that informs slave genealogical research.
And so the focus of research must always to some extent be on the slaveowner. Probate records are important tools in this process. As valued parts
of an estate, slaves were sometimes mentioned by name or may have been
referred to as having been inherited from another family member or else
purchased from a particular party.

For example, one David C. Moore of Duplin County, North Carolina
died in late 1863 or early 1864, leaving to his son Thomas "one half of that
portion of my negroes known as Megee Negroes including Martha & her
three children excepting those that I purchased from Thomas H. Megee
namely Aaron, Mary & three children."[11] Note that slaves were specifically
identified only insofar as the identification served the purposes of the testator. Therefore, slaves can be identified in a will by name and by family,
or else can be subsumed as simply an anonymous portion of a slaveholding. Generally speaking, the smaller the number of slaves in an estate, the
more likely there will be some sort of identifying language in the will.

It is sometimes possible to trace a particular slave through two or more
wills. For example, the will of Thomas Byrd, of Somerset County,
Maryland was probated on 16 March 1757, leaving "a negro girl called
Nice" to his daughter Mary Byrd, later wife of Paul Dulany, whose will was
probated on 6 March 1773, leaving "one negro woman named Nice" to his
son Henry.[12] Interestingly, the reference to Nice in the two wills also provides evidence for relationship between the slaveowners.

Other probate documents may also be helpful, such as estate inventories drawn up to execute the terms of a will. Slaves are sometimes mentioned by name in such documents. Bills of sale may also be found among probate documents if, for example, slaves had to be sold in order to pay an estate's debts.

The location of wills in the slave states has been considerably aided in several instances by the indexing of these records on a statewide basis. Many such indexes have been published.[13] The Genealogical Society of Utah has microfilmed early extant wills for many of the counties in the Southern slave states, while at least one state, North Carolina, has instituted its own microfilming program. Thus, the consultation of these important documents will not necessarily be confined to viewing the originals in a county courthouse, although the researcher should do so whenever possible. In addition, abstracts or transcriptions of county wills are increasingly finding their way into print. In many of the more recent publications in this genre, references to slaves are retained and special slave indexes are included. The researcher of slave genealogy should approach such published will abstracts carefully. If the compiler of such a book has not included slave data, that fact should be readily apparent after a few minutes of examination. The researcher should then attempt to access microfilm of the records or plan a genealogical research trip to view the originals.

Deeds and Other Local Records

As with any genealogical research, the quest for African American ancestry requires one to become familiar with the records and record-keeping practices of the state and county in which one is conducting investigations. It may be discovered that references to slaves exist in a variety of local record groups. County deed books may contain, in addition to real estate transactions, documentation of slave sales. For example, in Deed Book F-6 of Warren County, Kentucky, one finds certification of a bill of sale, dated 15 July 1813, of $1,500 from Upshaw R. Massey to Jesse Kerby for four slaves: a man named Moses, a woman named Milly, and two boys named Aaron and Robert, respectively. Massey and his wife are to "reserve use of said slaves until their own deaths."[14] But caution should be exercised in interpreting some deed records, particularly deeds in, or of, trust. If a slave is named in such a deed, it does not necessarily mean that there was

Figure 6 - Detail of a farmer's account book, 1745-1799, showing births of slaves. Courtesy of the University of Virginia Special Collections.

		Age
Jean-Baptiste	digger	17
(Fandango)	digger	35
(Douilha)	digger	25
Jupiter	builder	30
Sans Chargrin	builder	30
Fazau	blacksmith	40
Elie Toussaint		45
Francois		50
Lucie	mulatta	45
Polidon	laborer	40
Remy	foreman	45
Lubin		40
Banadarme	digger	35
Jean	digger	30
Antoine	digger	30
Ret ( )	blacksmith's aid	30
Lucielle		20
Cupidon	digger	30
Laurent	builder	30
Augustine	gardener	30
Coffe		45

Figure 7 - Slaves conveyed in an 1805 sale of land to Jean Baptiste Provost (P. Pedesclaux, June 12, 1805, NONA) from the Historic Resource Study of Jean Lafitte Chalmette Unit, National Historical Park and Preserve/Louisiana (I 29.58/3:J34).

a change in ownership. In such instances the slave was used as collateral. If the debt for which the slave acted as collateral was eventually discharged, then he or she would remain the property of the original owner.

Court records in the antebellum slave states could document any number of situations involving slaves and their owners, some mundane, others revealing, if not tragic. The circuit court records of Estill County, Kentucky contain the following examples: the record of an inquisition on the body of Stephen, a slave who had died as a result of mistreatment, described in great detail by his owner, William P. Noland; a suit by the same William Noland in 1837 against one Joseph Cox over the purchase of "a negro boy named Henry" for $200, in which Noland asserts that the slave had rheumatism and was subject to fits; a case in 1846 in which there is testimony of a married white woman giving birth to a child fathered by a slave named Mark.[15]

Tax records can also contain references to slaves. In the 1787 "census" of Virginia—tax records viewed by genealogists as a "replacement" for the lost 1790 census of that state—slaves are referred to by name together with their owners in Mecklenburg and Surry counties.[16] The books of tithables for Norfolk County, Virginia provide another example, containing named listings of slaves with owners for much of the eighteenth century.[17]

As shown, documentation for the buying and selling of slaves can be found in a variety of official sources on the local level. Such documentation can, of course, also be found in private papers. A pilot project attempting to bring together such documentation from an array of sources was the Slave Bills of Sale Project of the African American Family History Association in Atlanta, Georgia. This project transcribed, indexed, and published two volumes of these documents.[18] The genealogical community can hope that similar efforts will be undertaken throughout the South.

Plantation Records

The personal papers of any slaveholder are likely to contain information on slaves, assuming the greater portion of them survived. Such papers may still be in the possession of the family or else may have been deposited with a local or state historical society. Many records have also been deposited at research libraries.

As a genre of personal records, so-called "plantation records" are often voluminous and unpredictable. As often as not, those portions, which have genealogical value, will make up a small portion of the whole and may be difficult to pinpoint. Yet we can gain some sense of the possibilities of these records for slave genealogy if we consider their context. They are business records which were usually kept with personal and family papers for the simple reason that the plantation was essentially a family business—a complex and often extensive enterprise which could become even more complex and extensive with new holdings added from dowries and inheritances. Accounts needed to be kept for any number of things—the price of cotton needed to be monitored; the yield of a given acreage needed to be recorded; both needed to be considered in the context of the weather conditions from day to day and week to week. Loans and mortgages were a frequent concern, as were the affairs of tenants.

Intertwined with these concerns was the presence of slave labor on the plantation. Records of slaves can be found in several contexts. Clothes, blankets, or simply lengths of cloth were often issued on a regular basis to all slaves, and careful plantation owners kept good records of these distributions. Field hands were issued tools and implements and presumably held accountable for them. A plantation owner's "day book" may contain a variety of entries recording observations on the weather, livestock, and crops. It might also note the daily tasks undertaken on the plantation and which slaves were dispatched to fix a fence or deepen an irrigation channel. As property, slaves could also be mortgaged or rented—sometimes they were even insured—and careful records obviously had to be kept regarding such matters.

A child born of a slave mother became the property of the mother's owner, so it was in the owner's best interest to maintain a record of that birth in the absence of an official vital record. Therefore, in most cases the slaveowner's records may be the only place where slave birth records can be found. Deaths may also be recorded, although the reasons for doing so were less compelling. Many plantation owners maintained records outlining slave family groups, although, in some instances, one may find only a mother listed with her children. In such cases the identification of a slave father on a large plantation may be difficult.

These manuscript collections may also contain diaries and letters. The chance that important information concerning slaves would be contained in such items is admittedly slim, but not impossible. In letters and diaries, often written in faded and difficult-to-read handwriting, the mention of slaves by name may occur very infrequently, if at all. And if they are mentioned, their mention will not stand out in any appreciable fashion from the rest of the letter or diary. The whole letter or diary must be read with only a very limited realistic expectation of finding any information of genealogical value.

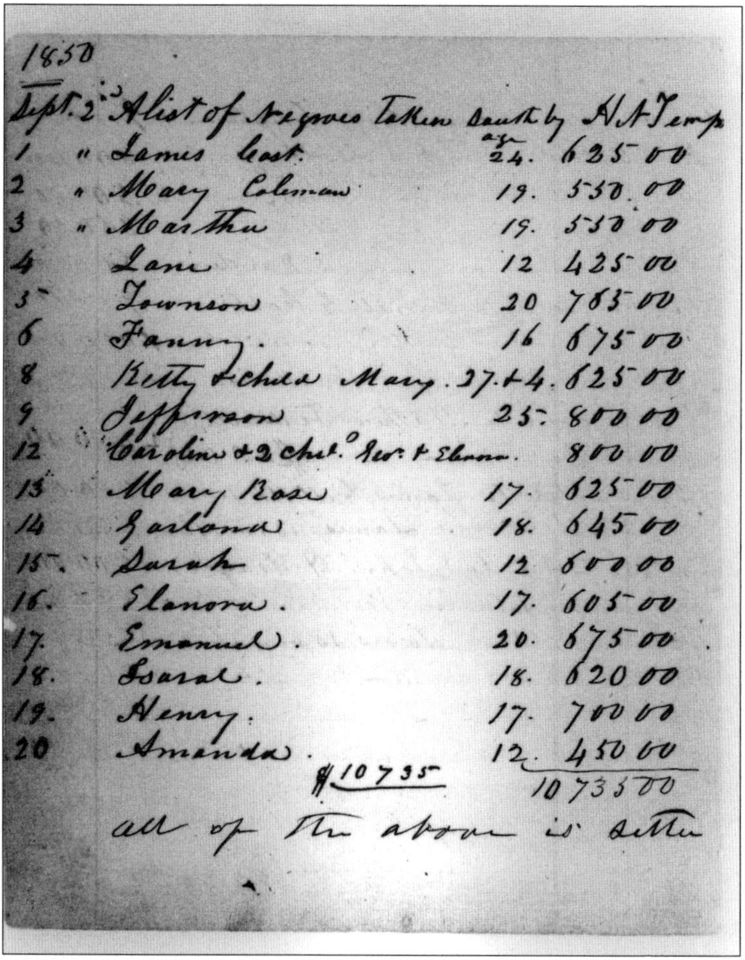
1850

Sept. 2nd A list of Negroes Taken South by H. A. Temp

1	" James East.	age 24.	625 00
2	" Mary Coleman	19.	550.00
3	" Martha	19.	550 00
4	Lane	12	425 00
5	Townson	20	785 00
6	Fanny.	16	675 00
8	Betty & child Mary.	27 & 4.	625 00
9	Jefferson	25.	800 00
12	Caroline & 2 chil.° Geo. & Elenor.		800 00
13	Mary Rose	17.	625 00
14	Garland	18.	645 00
15.	Sarah	12	600 00
16.	Elanora.	17.	605 00
17.	Emanuel.	20.	675 00
18.	Israel.	18.	620 00
19.	Henry.	17.	700 00
20	Amanda.	12.	450 00
	$10735		10735 00

all of the above is settled

Figure 8 - Detail of page from the *Templeman and Goodwin Slave Ledger, 1849-1857.* This record shows each slave's name, number of slaves on the plantation, their ages, as well as the price paid. Courtesy University of Virginia Special Collections.

The researcher should also bear in mind that a collection of papers will not necessarily be limited to one person, one generation, or even to a family of the same surname. As the plantation, or parts of it, were sold or transferred or willed to relations and in-laws, the records could also be transferred with the property. Thus, accumulations of plantation records could have a wide familial and geographical scope.

But how can the researcher examine these records? How can it be determined whether they exist? If they have been deposited in a library or historical society—and many of them have—there is a good chance that they have been registered in the *National Union Catalog of Manuscript Collections* (*NUCMC*), a serial reference work that first appeared in 1959 and has been for the most part published by the Library of Congress. *NUCMC* contains descriptions of manuscript collections held by hundreds of libraries throughout the country. It has also become far more user friendly with the publication of *Index to Personal Names in the National Union Catalog of Manuscript Collections 1959-1984* (Alexandria, Virginia: Chadwyk-Healey, 1988) and the creation of a Web site, <http://lcweb.loc.gov/coll/nucmc/>. The researcher of slave genealogy who has focused on a particular slaveholding family should consult the index to see if there are any listings in *NUCMC* for the papers of members of that family. Such a listing will indicate the repository at which they are held.[19]

There is also the possibility that records of interest have been microfilmed as part of the extensive microfilm series "Records of Ante-Bellum Southern Plantations From the Revolution Through the Civil War" (Frederick, Md.: University Publications of America, 1985-), edited by the noted historian Kenneth Stampp. This ongoing series is available at many research libraries and is accompanied by very thorough descriptions and reel guides for the component collections. The reel guides will reveal the likelihood of there being any records of interest in these collections, as well as their exact location in the microfilm.

Other Records of Slave Births and Deaths

During the antebellum period, keeping vital records had not yet been mandated by many state governments. For that simple reason, in many of the states, official vital records do not exist for slaves—or for anyone else—prior to the Civil War. Yet, as always, there are exceptions. For example,

Kentucky, in 1852, enacted legislation (repealed in 1862) requiring birth and death registrations in all counties. The birth records were to include children born to slave mothers, indicating date and place of birth, sex, and name of owner. A year later similar legislation was passed in Virginia. It has been noted that slaveowners may have been more intent on registering slave births than the births of their own children, a motivation likely arising from the need to protect property by an act of official registration.[20]

Similar motivations may have spurred the baptism of slaves by their owners. Such baptism records are often just as detailed as those for whites. The majority of such records, at least those which are extant, appear to be from Anglican/Episcopalian churches. Unfortunately, many of these registers have probably been lost, especially those of Virginia.[21] The situation is much better in South Carolina where the records of a number of Low Country churches survive, many extending well into the colonial era. These contain extensive slave baptismal records, some including the names of both slave parents as well as owners. The South Carolina Historical Society has microfilmed many of these records and made them available on microfiche. You can also search the society's online genealogy catalog at <http://www.historic.com/schs/>.

It has already been noted that the personal papers of slaveowners can contain records of slave births and deaths. At this juncture, it should also be mentioned that there is a possibility of slave births and deaths being noted in the slaveowner's Bible, together with those of his own family. To be sure, this was not a typical practice; however, when it did occur it likely reflected a small slaveholding, perhaps one or two slave families who had been in the possession of their owners for several decades.[22]

Runaway Slaves

Slaves sometimes attempted to escape from their owners. Some succeeded; most did not. Runaway slave advertisements, which usually contain physical descriptions and, occasionally, biographical information, can be of interest to the genealogist. In most cases, however, the identity of an ancestor's owner would have to be known for such an advertisement to be useful in compiling a family history. Many of these advertisements have been transcribed and published, most notably in Lathan A. Windley, *Runaway Slave Advertisements: A Documentary History From the 1730s to 1790, 4 vols.*

(Westport, Conn.: Greenwood, 1983), which covers the states of Virginia, North Carolina, Maryland, South Carolina, and Georgia. Robert K. Headley, *Genealogical Abstracts From the 18th Century Virginia Newspapers* (Baltimore: Genealogical Publishing Co., 1987), also contains runaway advertisements. Advertisements from eighteenth-century Pennsylvania are found in Gary T. Hawbaker, *Runaways, Rascals, and Rogues: Missing Spouses, Servants and Slaves. Abstracts from Lancaster County Pennsylvania Newspapers* (Hershey, Penn.: the author, 1987), and in Billy G. Smith and Richard Wojtowicz, *Blacks Who Stole Themselves: Advertisements for Runaways in the Pennsylvania Gazette 1728-1790* (Philadelphia: University of Pennsylvania, 1989). Also of interest is Helen Cox Tregillis, *River Roads to Freedom: Fugitive Slave Notices and Sheriff Notices Found in Illinois Sources* (Bowie, Md.: Heritage, 1988).

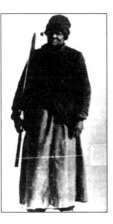

Figure 9 - "Stagecoach Mary" Fields, born a slave in Tennessee in 1832, likely a runaway, migrated to Montana and became the first female of any race to deliver mail by stagecoach. This picture was taken ca. 1900. Courtesy, Sunny Nash.

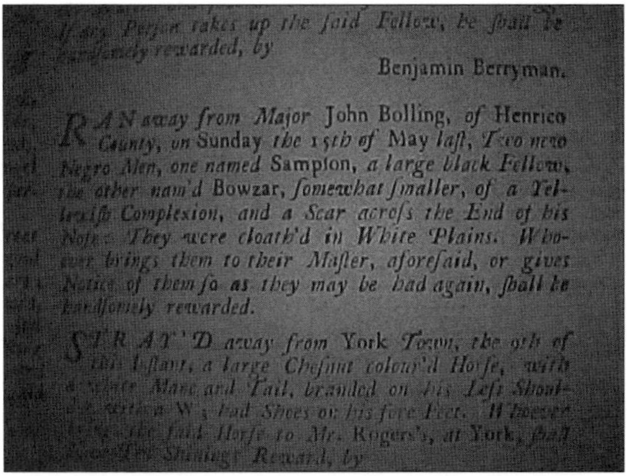

takes up the ſaid Fellow, he ſhall be ... rewarded, by

Benjamin Berryman.

RAN *away from Major* John Bolling, *of* Henrico *County, on* Sunday *the 15th of* May *laſt, Two new Negro Men, one named* Sampſon, *a large black Fellow, the other nam'd* Bowzar, *ſomewhat ſmaller, of a Yellowiſh Complexion, and a Scar acroſs the End of his Noſe. They were cloath'd in White Plains. Whoever brings them to their Maſter, aforeſaid, or gives Notice of them ſo as they may be had again, ſhall be handſomely rewarded.*

STRAY'D *away from* York *Town, the 9th of this Inſtant, a large Cheſnut colour'd Horſe, with a White Mane and Tail, branded on his Left Shoulder ... had Shoes on his fore Feet. Whoever ... the ſaid Horſe to Mr.* Rogers's, *at* York, *ſhall ... Reward, by*

Figure 10 - An example of a runaway slave advertisement from Windley, Lathan A., comp. *Runaway Slave Advertisements: A Documentary History from the 1730s to 1790.* 4 vols., Westport Conn., 1983 that appeared on The Virginia Runaways Project Web site <www.wise.virginia.edu/history/runaways/>.

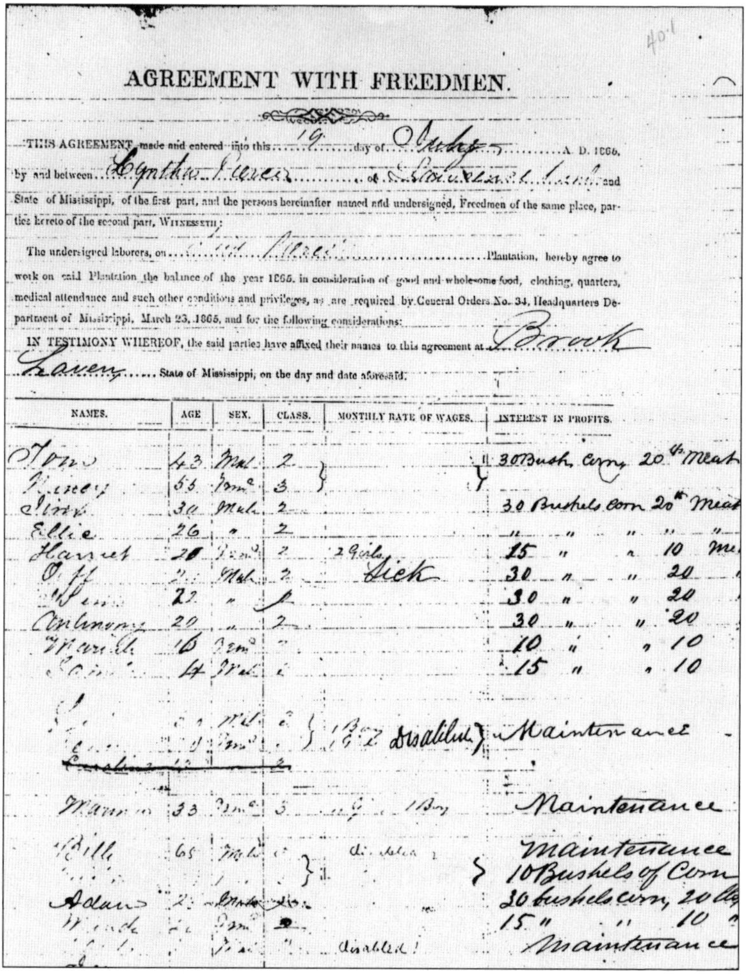

Figure 11 - An 1865 Freedmen's Agreement from Brookhaven, Mississippi.

The Bureau of Refugees, Freedmen, and Abandoned Lands

The Bureau of Refugees, Freedmen, and Abandoned Lands, usually referred to simply as the Freedmen's Bureau, was established by the federal government in 1865. The bureau was primarily concerned with assisting ex-slaves in their transition to life after slavery, although it also aided indigent whites shortly after the close of the war to some extent as well. Its activities among freed people were varied, including drawing up and enforcing labor contracts (figure 11), feeding the hungry, conducting marriages, leasing abandoned land, providing transportation, and, in general, presiding over Reconstruction policy. The bureau's records hold great genealogical potential; however, their contents elude a concise description. Records from Bureau headquarters in Washington, D.C. have been microfilmed but are not of much genealogical value. The next level down is that of the assistant commissioners, each one of whom presided over bureau activities in a given state, the only exception being the assistant commissioner for the District of Columbia. The following assistant commissioners' records have been microfilmed by the National Archives, in whose care they reside: Alabama (M809), Arkansas (M979), District of Columbia (M1055), Georgia (M798), Louisiana (M1027), Mississippi (M826), North Carolina (M843), South Carolina (M869), Tennessee (M999), Texas (M821), and Virginia (M1053).

Because of differences in record-keeping procedures, and possibly in the division of responsibility of record retention and storage between state headquarters and the field offices, their contents are by no means uniform. The contents also reflect a difference in the experiences of the state districts as well as the probability that more records survived from some states than from others.

The first fact the genealogist must understand is that the Freedmen's Bureau was not founded to create genealogically useful documents, and the same must be said for the microfilming of these records. Indeed, the records of the assistant commissioner for a given state may generally be without great genealogical utility. To get a sense of the contents of the records for a given district, consult "Black Studies: A Select Catalog of National Archives Microfilm Publications" (Washington, D.C.: National Archives, 1984). All of the district records contain correspondence and telegrams, as well as indexes to these documents. Much of these are intrabureau or intra-government communications so, as record groups, they hold little genealogical potential. The assistant commissioners' records will also contain various reports from the district field offices. Again, many of these will hold little of genealogical interest, although those reporting "outrages" (lynchings and other assaults upon African Americans) could be especially interesting, albeit somewhat chilling, to the genealogist. It should be noted that such reports, though generally a constant in district records, do not list a great many incidents.

Figure 12 - At right is the marriage license of Ned Peterson (above, holding hammer) and Etter Fuller (below, with child). Though the couple was actually married in 1910, this license was not filed until 1911. The photo of Ned shows him working on the railroad. The picture of Etter shows her at work as a housekeeper and baby sitter around 1912. Courtesy, Sunny Nash.

Of all the assistant commissioners' records, those for Mississippi hold the greatest genealogical potential. Only in Mississippi were local marriage registers included with the state district records. These are from Vicksburg, Davis Bend (just below Vicksburg), Natchez, and Meridian. These are among the most informative—and among the most poignant—of any American marriage records. Covering the years 1865 and 1866, these registers record the validation of "slave marriages" that occurred before emancipation and also record the marriages of men and women who were just beginning life together following the war. Although the names of parents are not provided, the racial identity of the bride and groom and their parents is one of the categories of information included. Often this description can be quite specific (for example, fraction of negro blood). Residence is also included, many of the men being Union soldiers, in which case a unit is indicated.

But probably the most important documents among the Mississippi assistant commissioner's records are the labor contracts. Most of these were implemented in 1865, the remainder being drawn up between 1866 and 1868. These agreements were primarily between ex-slaves and plantation owners throughout the state, although not every county is represented. Given the fact that all members of a freedman's family are usually mentioned by name, and the possibility that the contracts were executed with their former owners, the importance of these documents cannot be exaggerated. Many of the laborers are identified by given name and surname, although the majority are still represented only by a first name. The arrangement on microfilm of this extensive collection of documents will strike the researcher as haphazard; searching them is problematic. The arrangement is chronological, with instances of records for a given county being clumped together. The Mississippi Department of Archives and History has developed a microfiche index to these records.

Labor contracts are also found in the assistant commissioners' records for Arkansas and Tennessee, again ranging from 1865 to 1868. In the former, the arrangement is by year and alphabetically thereunder by name of employer. In the latter, the contracts are arranged in two sub-series, the first containing contracts in which the contracting parties were from Tennessee, with the arrangement being alphabetical by county and thereunder chronological. The second—and smaller—sub-series pertains to contracts with out-of-state employers.

Table 1. Microfilmed NARA Records of the Freedman's Savings and Trust Company

Roll No.	State	NARA Branch	Dates Covered
1	ALABAMA	HUNTSVILLE	28 NOV. 1865-21 AUG. 1874
2	ALABAMA	MOBILE	18 JUNE 1867-29 JUNE 1874
3	ARKANSAS	LITTLE ROCK	27 FEB. 1871-15 JULY 1874
4	WASHINGTON, D.C.	WASHINGTON	11 JULY 1865-30 DEC. 1871
5	WASHINGTON, D.C.	WASHINGTON	24 MAY 1872-22 JULY 1874
5	FLORIDA	TALLAHASSEE	25 AUG. 1866-15 JAN. 1872
6	GEORGIA	ATLANTA	15 JAN. 1870-15 JULY 1872
7	GEORGIA	AUGUSTA	23 NOV. 1870-29 JUNE 1874
8	GEORGIA	SAVANNAH	10 JAN. 1866-17 DEC. 1870
9	GEORGIA	SAVANNAH	17 DEC. 1870-22 OCT. 1872
10	GEORGIA	SAVANNAH	22 OCT. 1872-1 SEPT. 1874
11	KENTUCKY	LEXINGTON	21 MARCH 1870-3 JULY 1874
11	KENTUCKY	LOUISVILLE	15 SEPT. 1865-8 JULY 1874
12	LOUISIANA	NEW ORLEANS	20 JUNE 1866-29 JUNE 1874
12	LOUISIANA	SHREVEPORT	11 FEB. 1871-29 JUNE 1874
13	MARYLAND	BALTIMORE	3 MAY 1866-23 JUNE 1874
14	MISSISSIPPI	COLUMBUS	1 AUG 1870-16 JUNE 1874
14	MISSISSIPPI	NATCHEZ	29 MARCH 1870-18 JUNE 1874
15	MISSISSIPPI	VICKSBURG	28 JULY 1868-29 JUNE 1874
16	MISSOURI	ST. LOUIS	6 APRIL 1869-8 OCT. 1869
17	NEW YORK	NEW YORK CITY	20 FEB. 1871-6 JULY 1874
18	NORTH CAROLINA	NEW BERN	2 NOV. 1869-25 JULY 1874
18	NORTH CAROLINA	RALEIGH	9 APRIL 1868-20 APRIL 1868
18	NORTH CAROLINA	WILMINGTON	3 SEPT. 1869-30 OCT. 1869
19	PENNSYLVANIA	PHILADELPHIA	7 JAN. 1870-26 JUNE 1874
20	SOUTH CAROLINA	BEAUFORT	20 JUNE 1868-3 JULY 1874
21	SOUTH CAROLINA	CHARLESTON	19 DEC. 1865-2 DEC 1869
22	SOUTH CAROLINA	CHARLESTON	4 DEC. 1869-25 FEB. 1871
23	SOUTH CAROLINA	CHARLESTON	25 FEB. 1871-2 JULY 1872
24	TENNESSEE	MEMPHIS	28 DEC. 1865-1 JULY 1874
25	TENNESSEE	NASHVILLE	23 DEC. 1871-23 JUNE 1874
26	VIRGINIA	LYNCHBURG	8 JULY 1871-22 AUG. 1871
26	VIRGINIA	NORFOLK	4 DEC. 1871-29 JUNE 1874
27	VIRGINIA	RICHMOND	21 JUNE 1870-29 JUNE 1874

Another useful source is the collection of transportation records from the assistant commissioner for the District of Columbia. Following the Civil War, many ex-slaves were attempting to reunite with family members separated by circumstances of slavery or war, and many were assisted by the bureau. The extensive records for transportation assistance from Washington, D.C. provide evidence for journeys to places as far away as Wisconsin.

The researcher who is contemplating the use of the Freedmen's Bureau records should always take into account the possible mobility of the people under study. Many freed people from Virginia and Maryland received transportation out of Washington, just as, for example, many ex-slaves from the Louisiana side of the Mississippi River were married in Vicksburg, Davis Bend and Natchez, Mississippi.

The next level below that of the assistant commissioners' records is that of the field offices. With the exceptions of the records of the Arkansas field

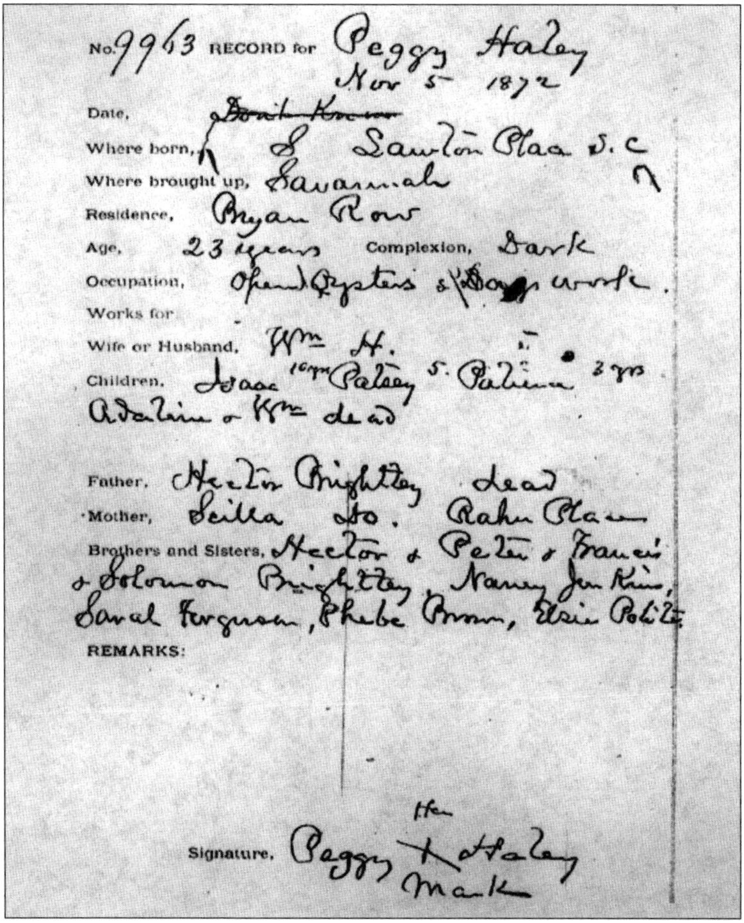
No. 9963 RECORD for Peggy Haley
Nov 5 1872
Date, ~~Don't Know~~
Where born, S Sawton Plaa S.C
Where brought up, Savannah
Residence, Bryan Row
Age, 23 years Complexion, Dark
Occupation, Open Oysters & Days work.
Works for
Wife or Husband, Wm H.
Children, Isaac 10 yrs Patsey 5. Patience 3 yrs
Adaline & Wm dead
Father, Hector Brightley dead
Mother, Scilla do. Rahn Plan
Brothers and Sisters, Hector & Peter & Francis & Solomon Brightley, Nancy Jenkins, Sarah Ferguson, Phebe Brown, Elsie Politz
REMARKS:
Signature, Peggy her x Haley mark

Figure 13 - From the Register of Signatures of depositors in branches of the Freedman's Savings and Trust Company, Savannah, Georgia.

offices and portions of the field office records from Louisiana and Tennessee, these materials have not been microfilmed and exist only in the form of the original documents stored at the National Archives. A final description of these records has yet to be published; however, a preliminary inventory was generated in 1973 and can be found in some genealogical libraries.[23] As with the state records, the contents of the field office records can vary considerably. It is probable that the proportion of genealogically useful records is much higher in the field office records than in the records of the assistant commissioners. If at all possible, the researcher should consult the preliminary inventory to determine, first of all, whether there are any field records for the localities under consideration and whether the records being described would have any genealogical potential. For example, any labor contracts or records of apprenticeship or marriage should be of interest.

The Freedman's Savings and Trust

The Freedman's Savings and Trust Company was incorporated in 1865 by act of Congress as a banking system for ex-slaves. Although it failed in 1874, it had by that time established thirty-three branches, mostly in Southern and Border states. The National Archives has microfilmed two record groups generated by the Freedman's Savings and Trust, although both are incomplete. Table 1 (page 22) shows the contents of these record groups.

Of the two record groups, the so-called signature records (National Archives microfilm publication M816) hold the most interest for the genealogist. These records were completed upon opening an account. The forms provided for a thorough identification of the depositor as well as the identification of family members in the event of the depositor's death. Their format varied among branches, and differing formats can also be found within the records of some individual branches. The extent to which the forms were completed also varies.

Nevertheless, these records often provide information not easily found elsewhere, if at all. For example, a seamstress and washerwoman named Nancy Patterson is shown to have established an account in the Louisville branch on 15 September 1865. In the final remarks portion of the signature record it is noted that she "formerly belonged to Bob Smith, was bot [sic] by her mother upon the block in 1854 or 5."[24] No relatives were noted in her record; however, it is not unusual to find three generations chronicled in a single instance. Typical of such an entry is that for Elias Webb, who held an account in the Vicksburg, Mississippi branch. His record states that he was born and raised in Anderson District, South Carolina, and was currently residing in Port Gibson, Mississippi. His father was Moses, his mother Rachel. He had four brothers, listed as Green Webb, Jeremiah Webb, Marcus Webb, and Scipio Lewis. His sisters were listed as Emeline, Mary, and Amanda Webb.[25] It was not unusual for people to cross a county line to make a deposit in a branch office. Therefore, while the number of cities with branches was limited, those branches served more than just the immediate vicinity. The signature records indicate that significant numbers of ex-slaves from at least ten Mississippi counties and three Louisiana parishes opened accounts at the Vicksburg branch.

Many of the signature record forms contained space to indicate regiment and company, evidence of the fact that soldiers of the United States Colored Troops were especially encouraged to set aside portions of their pay in Freedman's Savings and Trust accounts. Many did, and several instances of deposits made by soldiers on garrison duty in 1865 and 1866 can be found. Veterans continued to provide this information for many years after they had been mustered out.

The other partial record group which has been microfilmed is the index to the deposit ledgers (National Archives microfilm M817). Unfortunately, the deposit ledgers themselves have apparently not survived. An examination of the deposit ledger index may provide evidence of a signature record for a given individual in a particular branch; however, the signature records themselves are incomplete for many branches. The deposit ledger indexes are sometimes misidentified as indexes to the signature records; indeed, occasionally the deposit ledger number is the same as the signature register number. Even so, this happy coincidence cannot be relied upon, and the researcher who is interested in the signature records should be resigned to a frame-by-frame examination of the microfilm.

MILITARY RECORDS

There are many documented instances of African Americans serving the revolutionary cause during the American Revolution.[26] For example, compiled service record files can also be found, often simply under a given name, for slaves whose services as teamsters had been donated by their owners during the War of 1812. But the most important military records for African American genealogy are those created as a result of Civil War service. Along with the records of the Freedmen's Bureau and the Freedman's Savings and Trust, the service and pension records of African Americans who served in Union regiments focus on the most critical

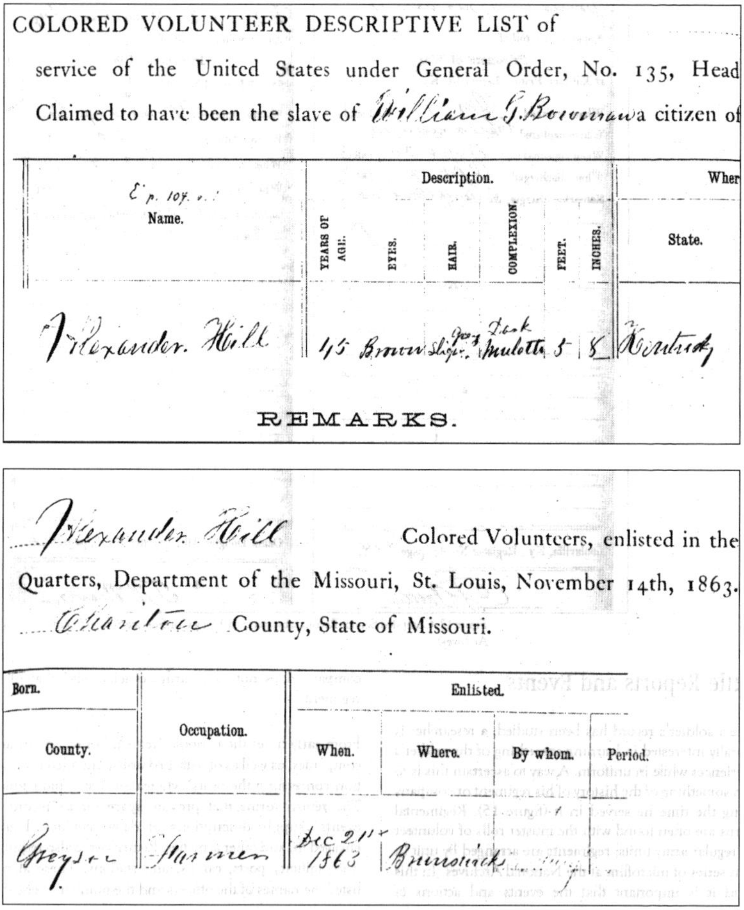

COLORED VOLUNTEER DESCRIPTIVE LIST of .... Colored Volunteers, enlisted in the service of the United States under General Order, No. 135, Head Quarters, Department of the Missouri, St. Louis, November 14th, 1863. Claimed to have been the slave of William G. Bowman a citizen of Chariton County, State of Missouri.

Name.	Description.						Where born.		Occupation.	Enlisted.			
	Years of age.	Eyes.	Hair.	Complexion.	Feet.	Inches.	State.	County.		When.	Where.	By whom.	Period.
Alexander Hill	45	Brown	Gray slight	Dark Mulatto	5	8	Kentucky	Greyson	Farmer	Dec 21st 1863	Brunswick		

REMARKS.

Figure 14 - Descriptive List Entry for a Former Slave Who Enlisted in the Union Army—Civil War. (top: left-hand page; bottom: right-hand page. Courtesy National Archives)

period for African American genealogy: the Civil War and Reconstruction. As such, they often hold important information concerning the experience of an individual or family during the final years of slavery.

Americans have recently become more aware of the role played by African American soldiers in the Civil War. The renowned 54th Massachusetts Volunteer Infantry was raised by that state and maintained its state numerical designation; however, the vast majority of regiments, eventually containing more than 170,000 African Americans, were recruited as federal regiments in the United States Colored Troops (USCT). Some regiments were raised under state sponsorship but eventually integrated into the USCT system and given USCT numerical designations. Recruits for these regiments came from a variety of circumstances. Some were free blacks who joined regiments raised in the North. Others were slaves from Border states that had not seceded. Under these circumstances their owners "volunteered" their services in exchange for the bounty which would normally have gone to the recruit. A third group comprised those who joined USCT regiments in the South after abandoning their former owners in areas under Union control.

As military service and pension records are covered elsewhere in this volume, they are not discussed in great detail here; however, some special considerations are worth mentioning. There is an index to the Civil War service records of USCT and other African American servicemen (National Archives Microfilm Publication M589). For many researchers this source will be critical in identifying veteran ancestors and in requesting their service and pension records. In most instances, especially when dealing with a common name, it will be helpful to consult Frederick H. Dyer, *Compendium of the War of the Rebellion* (Reprint. Dayton, Ohio: Morningside, 1978), which contains brief histories of all Union regiments, stating where they were organized and where they served. This information will often enable the researcher to identify an ancestor's regiment. For example, if the researcher had an ancestor from Tennessee and it was discovered that three soldiers with his name were on the rolls of three separate regiments, consulting Dyer's work might indicate that only one of those regiments was raised in Tennessee. The researcher would then be able to request the correct records from the National Archives.

Published Rosters and Indexes for African American Regiments in the Civil War

There is no published roster series for all USCT regiments; however, many rosters have been printed, usually as part of state roster publications. When taken together, they probably account for close to forty percent of all African Americans who served the Union cause. These are noted below; they may serve as an additional aid in identifying an ancestor's regiment.

Connecticut

See *Catalogue of Connecticut Volunteer Organizations* (Hartford, Conn.: Adjutant General, 1869) for rosters of the 29th Connecticut Volunteer Infantry and the 30th Connecticut Volunteer Infantry (later the 31st United State Colored Infantry).

Illinois

See *Illinois Adjutant General's Report*, vol. 8 (Springfield, Ill.: Adjutant General, 1886), for a roster of the 29th United States Colored Infantry.

Indiana

See *Indiana Adjutant General's Report*, vol. 7 (Indianapolis, Ind.: Adjutant General, 1865-1869), for a roster of the 28th United States Colored Infantry.

Iowa

See *Roster and Record of Iowa Soldiers in the War of the Rebellion Together With Historical Sketches of Volunteer Organizations 1861-1866* (Des Moines, Iowa: Emory English, state printer, 1911), for the First Regiment of Iowa African Infantry, later the 60th United States Colored Infantry.

Kansas

See *Kansas Adjutant General's Report* (Reprint. Topeka, Kans.: Hudson, 1896) for rosters of the 1st and 2nd Kansas Colored Volunteer Infantry (later the 79th and 83rd United States Colored Infantry, respectively), the 1st, 2nd, and 3rd Kansas Colored Light Artillery, and the Independent Colored Kansas Battery.

Kentucky

See the *Report of the Adjutant General of the State of Kentucky, vol. 2* (Frankfort, Ky.: Adjutant General, 1867), for rosters of the 5th and 6th United States Colored Cavalry; the 100th, 107th, 108th, 109th, 114th, 115th, 116th, 117th, 118th, 119th, 122nd, 123rd, 124th, and 125th United States Colored Infantry regiments; and the 8th, 12th, and 13th United States Colored Heavy Artillery.

Maryland

See L. Allison Wilmer, et al., *History and Roster of Maryland Volunteers, War of 1861-5, vol. 2* (Reprint. Silver Spring, Md: Family Line Publications in conjunction with Toomey Press, 1987), for rosters of the 4th, 7th, 9th, 19th, 30th, and 39th United States Colored Infantry regiments.

Massachusetts

See *Massachusetts Soldiers, Sailors and Marines in the Civil War, vol. 4* (Brookline, Mass.: Adjutant General, 1931-1935), for rosters of the 54th and 55th Massachusetts Volunteer Infantry regiments; and vol. 6 for a roster of the 5th Massachusetts Volunteer Cavalry.

Michigan

See *Record of Service of Michigan Volunteers in the Civil War, vol. 46*, for a roster of the 1st Michigan Colored Infantry (later the 102nd United States Colored Infantry).

North Carolina

See A.H. Stein, *History of the Thirty-Seventh Regiment United States Colored Infantry* (Philadelphia, Pa.: King and Baird, 1866), for a roster of this regiment, originally designated the 3rd North Carolina Colored Infantry.

Ohio

See the *Official Roster of the Soldiers of the State of Ohio in the War of the Rebellion* for rosters of the 127th Ohio Volunteer Infantry (later the 5th United States Colored Infantry) and the 27th United States Colored Infantry.

Pennsylvania
See Samuel P. Bates, *History of Pennsylvania Volunteers*, for rosters of the 3rd, 6th, 8th, 22nd, 24th, 25th, 32nd, 41st, 43rd, 45th, and 127th United States Colored Infantry regiments.

Rhode Island
See *Adjutant General's Report* (Providence, Rhode Island: Adjutant General, 1866) for a roster of the 14th Rhode Island Heavy Artillery (later the 8th and then the 11th United States Colored Heavy Artillery).

Tennessee
See *Tennesseans in the Civil War* (Nashville, Tenn.: Civil War Commission, 1965), which indexes troops in all Tennessee federal regiments, including the 11th (new), 12th, 13th, 14th, 15th, 16th, 17th, 40th, 42nd, 44th, 59th, 61st, 88th (new), and 101st United States Colored Infantry regiments, as well as batteries of the 2nd United States Colored Light Infantry and the 1st, 2nd, and 3rd United States Colored Heavy Artillery.

Other Military Sources

As noted previously, slaveowners in the Border states sometimes collected bounties when their slaves joined USCT regiments. Records for this bounty may be found in the soldier's service record, hence making the service record far more valuable than is usually the case.

Civil War veterans often submitted affidavits for their comrades in support of pension claims. The writing of affidavits was often a reciprocal affair, and a network of veterans from the same company often wrote affidavits for one another. Taken as a totality, the pension affidavits can on occasion reveal a common background for the pension applicants. This could be particularly important in the research of USCT veterans, as such an approach could uncover veterans from the same locality or even the same plantation who enlisted together. Obtaining the pension files of the fellow veterans who supplied affidavits for an ancestor's application may be costly but could in the end be very revealing.

Just prior to the end of the Civil War, the Confederate government adopted a policy for the use of slave soldiers; however, the policy change came too late for meaningful enactment, and no African Americans actually served as soldiers for the Southern cause. Even so, many slaves acted as body servants to their owners or to the sons of their owners when they entered Confederate service. Such service often qualified the servants for pensions paid to Southern veterans by the former states of the Confederacy. Some were even able to find a place in retirement homes for Confederate veterans.

Many slaves were drafted by the Confederate government for manual labor, perhaps with compensation for their owners. Documentation for such labor arrangements is not centralized but does occasionally surface in private papers or government archives. Similar documentation may also be found from the Union side, such as the recent publication of a list of slaves impressed for work on the Nashville and North Western Railroad in October 1863.[27] These particular records are especially important because they supply the name of owner together with the residence and a physical description of the slave.

CONCLUSION

In a general way, the major sources for African American genealogical research have been considered. There are others, many of them specific to particular states or localities. Again, the researcher must become thoroughly familiar with the records of a locality or state in order to fully exploit them.

Many major indexing and publication projects are still needed in this ever-expanding field. Until they are accomplished, the researcher of African American genealogy will often need to call upon deep reserves of patience and perseverance. The continued publication of county records holds great potential, but that potential could be squandered if the importance of such records to African American genealogy is ignored or overlooked. The clearest example discussed here is the transcription of the names of slaves mentioned in wills. Unfortunately, though, many local publishing cooperatives and programs systematically exclude African Americans from the records being published. Books or series purporting to record the cemeteries, the postbellum marriages, school censuses, and even the census schedules for a given county have appeared within the last fifteen years in a "whites only" format. The researcher of African American genealogy must be aware of this possibility, both in order to properly evaluate what is published and, perhaps, to exert pressure to see that such omissions are rectified.

By demonstrating the often surprising richness of many research sources for African American genealogy, it is hoped that more people will be encouraged to begin their research in this field, fully aware of the problems, yet at least a little heartened by the fact that the African American historical experience can be documented—at times in great detail—through the lives of the ancestors of present-day African Americans.

END NOTES

1. Among them the following: Dorothy A. Boyd-Rush, *Register of Free Blacks, Rockingham County, Virginia, 1807-1859* (Bowie, Md.: Heritage, 1992); Katherine G. Bushman, *Registers of Free Blacks, 1810-1864, Augusta County, Virginia and Staunton, Virginia* (Verona, Va.: Mid-Valley Press, 1989); Richard B. Dickinson, *Entitled! Free Papers in Appalachia Concerning Antebellum Freeborn Negroes and Emancipated Blacks in Montgomery County, Virginia* (Washington, D.C.: National Genealogical Society, 1981); Frances B. Latimer, *The Register of Free Negroes: Northampton County, Virginia, 1853 to 1861* (Bowie, Md.: Heritage, 1992); Dorothy S. Provine, Alexandria County, *Virginia Free Negro Registers 1797-1861* (Bowie, Md.: Heritage, 1990); and Donald Sweig, *Registrations of Free Negroes Commencing September Court 1822...* (Fairfax, Va.: Fairfax County History Commission, 1977).

2. Transcribed in Sweig, 97.

3. Wright State University, "Records of Black and Mulatto Persons. . . . A printed abstract of these records entitled Register of Blacks in the Miami Valley: A Name Abstract (1804-1857)" was compiled by Stephen Haller and Robert Smith.

4. See Herbert G. Gutman, *The Black Family in Slavery and Freedom, 1750-1925* (New York: Vintage Books, 1976), 230-56.

5. David T. Thackery, "Crossing the Divide: A Census Study of Slaves Before and After Freedom," *Origins* (Newberry Library) 2 (March 1989).

6. Gutman, 245.

7. Freedman's Savings and Trust Signature Books (National Archives Microfilm Publication M816). Vicksburg, Mississippi, branch, record no. 1288.

8. The use of the slave schedules as supporting documentation is amply demonstrated in David H. Streets, *Slave Genealogy: A Research Guide With Case Studies* (Bowie, Md.: Heritage, 1986), although, not surprisingly, their use is confined to small slaveholdings.

9. See Loretto Dennis Szucs, "Research in Census Records" in *The Source: A Guidebook of American Genealogy, Rev. ed.* (Salt Lake City, Utah: Ancestry, 1997).

10. A notable exception is found in Jonnie B. Arnold, Index to 1860 Mortality Schedule of South Carolina (Greenville, S.C.: the author,

1982). On the other hand, many of the indexes appearing on the National Archives microfilm publications of these schedules, as well as those published by Accelerated Indexing, should be treated with caution.

11. The abstract of this will (Duplin County will book, vol. 3, entry 85) can be found in William L. Murphy, *Genealogical Abstracts: Duplin County Wills, 1730-1860* (Rose Hill, N.C.: Duplin County, Historical Society, 1982), 120.

12. Wills, Maryland State Archives. Liber 30, folio 351, and liber 39, folio 521, respectively. I am indebted to my colleague Tony Hoskins for bringing this interesting example to my attention.

13. Among such published indexes: Jeannette Holland Austin, *Index to Georgia Wills* (Baltimore, Md.: Genealogical Publishing Co., 1985); Thornton W. Mitchell, *North Carolina Wills: A Testator Index 1665-1900*, "corrected and revised edition" (Baltimore, Md.: Genealogical Publishing Co., 1992); Byron and Barbara Sistler, *Index to Tennessee Wills & Administrations 1779-1861* (Nashville, Tenn.: Sistler, 1990); Clayton Torrence, *Virginia Wills and Administrations 1632-1800: An Index* (Richmond, Va.: National Society of Colonial Dames of America, 1930); Betty Couch Wiltshire, *Mississippi Index of Wills* (Bowie, Md.: Heritage, 1989).

14. Abstracted in Joyce Martin Murray, *Deed Abstracts of Warren County, Kentucky 1812-1821* (Dallas, Tex.: Murray, 1986), 12.

15. Abstracted by Ellen and Diane Rogers, *Estill County, Kentucky, Circuit Court Records* (Irvine, Kent.: the compilers, 1984), vol. 1, pp. 3, 7; vol. 2, p. 240.

16. Transcribed in Nettie Schreiner-Yentis, *The 1787 Census of Virginia* (Springfield, Va.: Genealogical Books in Print, 1987).

17. See Elizabeth N. and W. Bruce Wingo, *Norfolk County, Virginia Tithables 1730-1750* (Norfolk, Va.: the compilers, 1979), and *Norfolk County, Virginia Tithables 1751-1765* (Norfolk, Va.: the compilers, 1981).

18. *Slave Bills of Sale Project* (Atlanta, Ga.: African-American Family History Association, 1986).

19. See Kory L. Meyerink, "Databases, Indexes, and Other Finding Aids" in *The Source: A Guidebook of American Genealogy*, Rev. ed. (Salt Lake City: Ancestry, 1997).

20. Johni Cerny, "Black Ancestral Research" in *The Source: A Guidebook of American Genealogy, 1st ed.* (Salt Lake City: Ancestry, 1984).

21. One which has survived and which contains extensive slave birth and baptism listings was transcribed and published in 1897 and was reprinted recently: The Parish Register of Christ Church, Middlesex County, Va. From 1653 to 1812 (Easley, S.C.: Southern Historical Society, 1988).

22. For example, see Hugh Buckner Johnston, Jr., "Some Bible and Other Family Records," *North Carolina Genealogical Society Journal* 7 (4) (November 1981).

23. Preliminary Inventory of the Records of the Field Offices of the Bureau of Refugees, Freedmen and Abandoned Lands (Washington, D.C.: National Archives and Records Service, 1973). For a sense of the potential found in many of these more local records, the researcher may wish to consult an essay by Barry Crouch and Larry Madras: "Reconstructing Black Families: Perspectives From the Texas Freedmen's Bureau Records," in *Our Family, Our Town: Essays on Family and Local History Sources in the National Archives* (Washington, D.C.: National Archives and Records Service, 1987).

24. Freedman's Savings and Trust Signature Books. Louisville, Kentucky, branch, record no. 1.

25. *Ibid.*, Vicksburg, Mississippi branch, record no. 1186.

26. See Robert Ewell Greene, *Black Courage 1775-1783: Documentation of Black Participation in the American Revolution* (Washington, D.C.: National Society of the Daughters of the American Revolution, 1984).

27. Gale Williams Bamman, "African-Americans Impressed for Service on the Nashville and North Western Railroad, October 1863," National *Genealogical Society Quarterly* 80 (3) (September 1992). Although this particular record is found in the Tennessee State Library and Archives, Bamman notes that similar records can be found in National Archives Record Groups 92 (Quartermaster General's Office), 94 (Adjutant General's Office), and 109 (Captured Confederate Records).

BIBLIOGRAPHY

Historical Background

Berlin, Ira. *Slaves Without Masters: The Free Negro in the Antebellum South.* New York: Oxford University Press, 1976.

Berlin, Ira, et al., eds. *Freedom: A Documentary History of Emancipation 1861-1867 Selected From the Holdings of the National Archives of the United States.* New York: Cambridge University Press, 1982-.

Cornish, Dudley Taylor. *The Sable Arm: Black Troops in the Union Army, 1861-1865.* Lawrence: University Press of Kansas, 1956.

Foner, Eric. *Reconstruction: America's Unfinished Revolution, 1863-1877.* New York: Harper & Row, 1988.

Gray, Deborah. *Ar'nt I a Woman? Female Slaves in the Plantation South.* New York: W.W. Norton, 1985.

Grossman, James R. *Land of Hope: Chicago, Black Southerners, and the Great Migration.* Chicago: University of Chicago Press, 1989.

Hawbaker, Gary T. *Runaways, Rascals, and Rogues: Missing Spouses, Servants and Slaves. Abstracts From County Pennsylvania Newspapers.* Hershey, Pa: the author, 1987.

Gutman, Herbert. *The Black Family in Slavery and Freedom, 1750-1925.* New York: Vintage Books, 1976.

Litwack, Leon F. *North of Slavery: The Negro in the Free States 1790-1860.* Chicago: University of Chicago Press, 1961.

Smith, Billy G., and Richard Wojtowicz. *Blacks Who Stole Themselves: Advertisements for Runaways in the Pennsylvania Gazette 1728-1790.* Philadelphia: University of Pennsylvania, 1989.

Windley, Lathan A. *Runaway Slave Advertisements: A Documentary History From the 1730s to 1790.* 4 vols. Westport, Conn.: Greenwood, 1983.

Guides and Bibliographies

Black Studies: A Select Catalog of National Archives Microfilm Publications. Washington, D.C.: National Archives, 1984.

Cerny, Johni, and Arlene Eakle. *Ancestry's Guide to Research: Case Studies in American Genealogy.* Salt Lake City: Ancestry, 1985. One of the case studies is African American.

Dyer, Frederick H. *Compendium of the War of the Rebellion.* Reprint. Dayton, Ohio: Morningside, 1978.

Headley, Robert K. *Genealogical Abstracts From the 18th Century Virginia Newspapers.* Baltimore: Genealogical Publishing Co., 1987.

Index to Personal Names in the National Union Catalog of Manuscript Collections 1959-1984. Alexandria, Virginia: Chadwyk-Healey, 1988.

Records of Ante-Bellum Southern Plantations From the Revolution Through the Civil War. Frederick, Md.: University Publications of America, 1985-.

Rose, James, and Alice Eichholz. *Black Genesis.* Detroit: Gale Research Co., 1978.

Streets, David H. *Slave Genealogy: A Research Guide with Case Studies.* Bowie, Md.: Heritage, 1986.

Thackery, David T. *A Bibliography of African American Family History at the Newberry Library.* Chicago: The Newberry Library, 1993.

_____, and Dee Woodtor. *Case Studies in Afro-American Genealogy.* Chicago: The Newberry Library, 1989.

Tregillis, Helen Cox. *River Roads to Freedom: Fugitive Slave Notices and Sheriff Notices Found in Illinois Sources.* Bowie, Md.: Heritage, 1988.

Turpin, Joan. *Register of Black, Mulatto and Poor Person in Four Ohio Counties 1791-1861.* Bowie, Md.: Heritage Books, 1985.

Representative Genealogies and Family Histories

Johnson, Michael P., and James L. Roark. *Black Masters: A Free Family of Color in the Old South.* New York: W.W. Norton, 1984.

Lucas, Ernestine Grant. *From Paris to Springfield: The Slave Connection Basye-Basey.* Decorah, Iowa: Anundsen, 1983.

Madden, T.O., Jr., and Ann L. Miller. *We Were Always Free. The Maddens of Culpeper County, Virginia: A 200-Year Family History.* New York: Norton, 1992.

Patterson, Ruth Polk. *The Seed of Sally Good'n: A Black Family of Arkansas 1833-1953.* Lexington: University Press of Kentucky, 1985.

Pinkard, Ophelia Taylor. *Taylors of Northumberland County, Virginia.* Washington, D.C.: Pinkard, 1987.

Redford, Dorothy Spruill. *Somerset Homecoming: Recovering a Lost Heritage.* New York: Doubleday, 1988.

White, Barnetta McGhee. *In Search of Kith and Kin: The History of a Southern Black Family.* Baltimore: Gateway, 1986.

AFRICAN AMERICAN CASE STUDIES

by Johni Cerny, BS, FUGA

Discovering American-born ancestors back to the end of the Civil War can be accomplished without encountering too many obstacles, but some exceptions always exist. Those of African American descent may hit some snags when a former slave family changed its name a number of times before making a final choice or when a mother's children had different fathers and did not share the same surname. Tracing slave families before they were freed requires the African American genealogist to look for their ancestors in records created by the families who enslaved them.

The two case studies presented here serve to demonstrate the basics of genealogical research and show that tracing slaves, without exception is difficult. Few research problems involving slave ancestry are alike, but methods employed in one case often can be applied in others. The methods used in these studies are not the only approaches for solving research problems such as these. The goal here is to present some typical cases that involve using a variety of records to generate as much information as possible about a slave family and its descendants.

Case Study 1
From Sarah to Nelson Wells—Tracing African American Families through the Post-Emancipation Period

The families discussed here are the progenitors of the American musician, composer, and arranger Quincy Jones. After writing the musical score for *Roots,* the television mini-series adapted from Alex Haley's epic novel, Quincy wanted to learn more about his own ancestors. He hired my staff and I to trace his ancestry and this synopsis of our research is offered as a guide for others just beginning their search.

Quincy's mother, Sarah Frances Wells, was the fifth of eleven children born to Love Adam Wells and Mary Bell Lanier. Sarah and her siblings recalled people and events from the past, but had not attempted to verify names, dates of birth, marriage, and death, or prove family relationships. Interviews with family members play a vital role in compiling family histories and genealogies. It's important to interview aged relatives while their memory is sharp and accurate. Prepare questions and send them ahead so relatives can prepare their answers in advance. Use a video recorder whenever possible. If not, take two recording devices (in case one malfunctions) and extra batteries. Make sure you take writing materials along. If you can't interview relatives in person, send the list ahead and arrange a time for a telephone interview. Let them know if you're planning to tape the conversation. It's not easy to compile a list of standard questions. Everyone you interview will be unique and some will require more than the standard questions discussed here.

Sometimes new questions will surface during the interview. Jot them down and ask them later, rather than interrupt the flow of the interview. Ideally, it would be great if you could interview every living relative, but with families spread all over the globe it might be impossible. It's a good idea to start with the oldest members of your immediate and extended family. When relatives who could answer important questions are deceased, turn to their children and friends, especially their childhood friends. Obtaining names, dates, places, and relationships isn't the only purpose of interviewing relatives. Record their memories of people and events! The information obtained from relatives and friends of the family should be used to piece together a family group. Any facts provided from someone's memory must be documented so that when information is shared with others or published, no one will question the accuracy of the family tree! Members of the Wells family were interviewed and asked to provide copies of important documents in their possession, such as birth, marriage and death certificates, record pages from family Bibles, obituary notices, funeral cards, and military records.

Documenting the history of the Wells family began with an telephone interview and ended after 300 hours of research. The interview with Quincy's Aunt Mable Dulaney on June 12, 1983 produced some solid facts and several dozen clues to follow when tracking down information about her brothers and sisters. She also sent a photocopy of a list of births from the family's Bible. Each entry on the list appears to have been made by the same person with the same pen, which suggests that they were not made at the time of each child's birth. The list of births, along with the details Mable gave about her family, could be used as to create a preliminary family group, but both had to be supported from facts recorded in original records.

Preliminary Family Group

Love Adam Wells
born in Vicksburg, Mississippi
died 3 April 1948 in St. Louis, Missouri
married on 24 August 1895 in Vicksburg, Mississippi

Mary Bell Lanier
daughter of James Lanier (a white man) and Cordelia Dickson
born 7 August 1879 in rural Bovina near Vicksburg
died 13 October 1960 in St. Louis

Mable Dulaney nee Wells stated in an interview that her mother was the illegitimate daughter of James Balance Lanier, son of Needham Burch Lanier (a spy for the Confederacy) and Cordelia Dickson. Mary told her children that even though her parents never married, James Lanier attended her wedding and admonished Love Wells to treat his daughter well.

Their children:
i. James L. Wells, born 12 January 1896 in Warren Co., Mississippi; died 10 November 1896 in Warren Co., Mississippi.
ii. John T. Wells, born 1 February 1897 in Warren Co., Mississippi; died 26 July 1949 in St. Louis, Missouri. He married Mozella (maiden surname unknown).
iii. Leonia Gertrud Wells, born 12 January 1900 in Vicksburg, Mississippi; died 8 November 1971 in Chicago, Illinois. She married Benjamin Hill in Hollandale, Mississippi.
iv. Andrew Nelson Wells, born 29 August 1901 in Vicksburg, Mississippi; died 2 January 1953 in St. Louis, Missouri. Married and divorced, but family had nothing more about him or his descendants.
v. Sarah Frances Wells, born 31 July 1903 in Bovina, Warren Co., Mississippi. She married Quincy Delight Jones, Sr. on 8 October 1932 in Milwaukee, Wisconsin. They divorced.

vi.   Mealure "Amelia" Jean Wells, born 28 January 1905 in Vicksburg, Mississippi; died 29 March 1975 in St. Louis, Missouri. She changed her name from Mealure to Amelia. Married Herman Bell in 1926 in St. Louis, Missouri.

vii.   Otho Henry Wells, born 18 October 1906 in Vicksburg, Mississippi; died in February 1958 in Detroit, Michigan. He married Geraldine (maiden surname unknown). They divorced and he married at least once more, but the details of that marriage are unknown.

viii.   Mabel Lois Wells, born 15 January 1909 in Vicksburg, Mississippi. She married John Wallace Dulaney on 22 November 1945 in St. Louis, Missouri.

ix.   Jennie Joyce Wells, born 20 September 1910 in Vicksburg, Mississippi; died on 15 November 1975 in St. Louis, Missouri. She married (1) Charles Burrell and they divorced, (2) Mr. Lacy who died, and (3) Jimmy Lee.

x.   Liller Wells, born 15 March 1912 in Vicksburg, Mississippi; she died on 17 January 1967 in Chicago, Illinois.

xi.   Cleophas Wells, born 18 December 1913 in Vicksburg, Mississippi; died in St. Louis, Missouri. He married Helen Squires in St. Louis.

Using Public Records to Verify Information

Birth, marriage, and death records can attest to a person's identity, dates of events, age at the time of an event, parentage, residence, relationship to others, and various other facts. Called *vital records*, copies of these documents should be obtained whenever possible. The marriage record of Love Wells and Mary Lanier agrees with the information given in the interview. It states "Love Adam Wells and Mary B. Lanier, both of Vicksburg, Mississippi, were married on 24 August 1895 in Vicksburg by L. Lewensburg in the presence of Sarah Jenkins and others."[1]

Mississippi did not begin keeping birth and death records until 1913, the year Mary Wells gave birth to her youngest child. It took awhile before everyone complied with the new law requiring parents to register the birth of a child, which may explain why some births cannot be verified. Applicants for social security benefits who were born before birth records were required could file a "delayed birth registration." Death records are much easier to obtain and offer far more information than a birth record. The information found on each vital record obtained for members of the Wells family has been added to the *Updated Family Group* at the end of this study.

Census records also help researchers place people into family groups. Love Wells and his family were enumerated during the 1910 census in Warren County, Mississippi[2]:

Locality	1910 - Beat 4, Warren County, Mississippi							
ED, Sheet, Line	Enumeration District 69, Sheet 5, Line 71							
Enumeration Date	22 April 1910							

| Location | | | Description | | | | Birth Place | | |
House	Fam.	Name	Sex	Age	Relationship	Occupation	Self	Fath	Moth
95	96	Wells, Lovie	M	33	Head	Farmer	MS	MS	MS
		", Mable[sic]	F	30		Laborer	MS	MS	MS
		", John	M	13		School	MS	MS	MS
		", Leonie	F	10		School	MS	MS	MS
		", Sarah	F	7		School	MS	MS	MS
		", Amelia	F	5		School	MS	MS	MS
		", O	M	3		School	MS	MS	MS
		", Mable	F	1		School	MS	MS	MS

The census also states that Lovie and Mable (a phonetic corruption of Mary Bell) Wells had been married fourteen years and that she had given birth to eight children—of whom only seven were still living in 1910. They were renting a home with land to operate a small farm.

Love Wells was enumerated for the first time as married adult in the 1900 census of Warren County, Mississippi:[3]

Locality	1900 - Beat 4, Warren County, Mississippi						
ED, Sheet, Line	Enumeration District 135, Sheet 118A, Line 10						
Enumeration Date	7 June 1900						

| Location | | | | | | Birth Place | | |
House	Fam.	Name	Birth Date	Relationship	Occupation	Self	Fath	Moth
79	79	Wells, Love	Jan 1877	Head	Farming	MS	MS	MS
		" Mary	May 1889	Wife	Farming	MS	MS	MS
		" John	Jan 1897	Son		MS	MS	MS
		" Leone	Feb 1900	Daughter		MS	MS	MS

The 1900 census also states that Love and Mary Wells had been married for five years and that she had given birth to three children, of whom only two were living when the census was taken.

Identifying the parents of Love Wells was accomplished by searching two sources, his death certificate and the 1880 census. According to his death certificate, Love Wells was born on January 17, 1877 in Vicksburg, Mississippi, a son of Nelson Wells and Sarah Campbell—both of whom were born in Vicksburg. Love Wells died on April 3, 1948 at age seventy-one years, two months, and sixteen days from cerebral thrombosis after being treated for twenty-two days at the Homer G. Phillips Hospital in St. Louis, Missouri. He was buried five days later at Washington Park Cemetery. His widow, Mary Wells, provided the information recorded on the death certificate, which also states that she was sixty-eight years old at the time of his death.[4]

Nelson Wells and his family were living in the Bovina Precinct of Warren County, Mississippi when the 1880 census was taken:[5]

Locality	1880 - Bovina Precinct, Warren County, Mississippi
ED, Sheet, Line	Enumeration District 78, Page 14, Line 25
Enumeration Date	5 June 1880

Location			Description				Birth Place		
House	Fam.	Name	Sex	Age	Relationship	Occupation	Self	Fath	Moth
95	96	Nelson Wells	M	26		Farmer	MS	MS	MS
		Sarah "	F	23	Wife	Keeping House	MS	MS	MS
		Johnnie "	M	4	Son		MS	MS	MS
		Adam "	M	2	Son		MS	MS	MS

This census places Love Adam Wells in a family as a child and implies that his parents, Nelson Wells and Sarah were former slaves, viz. they were born before the Civil War began. The methods used to trace Nelson's ancestry and document his years as a slave are presented in the second case study.

Update

Family groups should be updated whenever new information surfaces. Most family historians use one of several excellent software programs designed to make updating quick and easy. Enter the source of every fact recorded so that when information is shared with others they can check it's accuracy.

Updated Family Group

Love Adam Wells
son of Nelson Wells and Sarah Campbell
born in 17 January 1877 in Vicksburg, Mississippi[6]
died 3 April 1948 in St. Louis, Missouri. According to his death certificate, Love Wells, son of Nelson Wells and Sarah Campbell, both of whom were born in Vicksburg, Mississippi, died at Homer O. Phillips Hospital from cerebral thrombosis at age 71 years, 2 months, and 16 days. Love Wells had been living at 3950 Enright Ave. (not Aldine as the record states) in St. Louis prior to being admitted to the hospital twenty-two days prior to his death. He was buried on April 8, 1948 at Washington Park Cemetery.[7]
married on 24 August 1895 in Vicksburg, Mississippi[8]

Mary Bell Lanier
daughter of James Lanier (a white man) and Cordelia Dickson
born 7 August 1879 in Vicksburg, Mississippi[9]
died 13 October 1960 in St. Louis, Missouri. Mary Wells died from acute heart failure and bronchial asthma. She was interred at Washington Park Cemetery on 18 October 1960.[10]

Mable Dulaney nee Wells stated in an interview that her mother was the illegitimate daughter of James Balance Lanier, son of Needham Burch Lanier (a spy for the Confederacy) and Cordelia Dickson. Mary told her children that even though her parents never married, James Lanier attended her wedding and admonished Love Wells to treat his daughter well.

Their children:
i.	James L. Wells, born 12 January 1896 in Warren Co., Mississippi;[11] died 10 November 1896 in Warren Co., Mississippi.[12]
ii.	John Thomas Wells, born 1 February 1897 in Warren Co., Mississippi;[13] died 26 July 1949 in St. Louis, Missouri. He married Mozella (maiden surname unknown).[14]
iii.	Leonia Gertrud Wells, born 12 January 1900 in Vicksburg, Mississippi; died 8 November 1971 in Chicago, Illinois. Her death certificate states that Leona Wells died at Mt. Sinai Hospital in Chicago from an

intra-cerebral hemorrhage caused by a cerebral contusion suffered the previous day (November 7, 1971) in a fall while a resident of a nursing home. Her parents are listed as Love Wells and Mary Lenear [sic]. The information on the certificate was provided by Mable L. Dulaney, sister of the deceased, who lived at 6753 South Evans Ave. in Chicago.[15] She married Benjamin Hill in Hollandale, Mississippi.

iv.   Andrew Nelson Wells, born 29 August 1901 in Vicksburg, Mississippi; died 2 January 1953 in St. Louis, Missouri. According to his death certificate, Andrew N. Wells died at Homer G. Phillips Hospital from a pulmonary embolism at age 50 years, 4 months, and 3 days. The information on the certificate was given by Mrs. Mary Wells (his mother) of 4323 Enright in St. Louis. Andrew, a divorced carpenter, was interred at Washington Park Cemetery (5500 Brown Road in St. Louis) on 7 January 1953.[16]

v.   Sarah Frances Wells, born 31 July 1903 in Vicksburg, Warren Co., Mississippi.[17] She married Quincy Delight Jones, Sr. on 8 October 1932 in Milwaukee, Wisconsin. They divorced. She died in October 1999.[18]

vi.   Mealure "Amelia" Jean Wells, born 28 January 1905 in Vicksburg, Mississippi;[19] died 29 March 1975 in St. Louis, Missouri. According to her death certificate, Amelia Jean Bell was dead on arrival at Homer Phillips Hospital in St. Louis, Missouri. She died from bronchial asthma at age 70. She was a widow and had been working at the Warfield Gift Shop. Her social security number is listed as 495-18-9664A. Amelia was buried at Washington Park Cemetery in St. Louis. Jennie Lee, her sister, gave the information on the death certificate.[20] She changed her name from Mealure to Amelia before reaching adulthood. Amelia married Herman Bell in 1926 in St. Louis, Missouri.

vii.   Otho Henry Wells, born 18 October 1906 in Vicksburg, Mississippi; died in February 1958 in Detroit, Michigan. He married Geraldine (maiden surname unknown). They divorced and he married at least once more, but the details of that marriage are unknown.

viii. Mable Lois Wells, born 15 January 1909 in Vicksburg, Mississippi. She married John Wallace Dulaney on 22 November 1845 in St. Louis, Missouri.[21]

ix. Jennie Joyce Wells, born 20 September 1910 in Vicksburg, Mississippi. Her delayed birth certificate states that she was born September 20, 1910 in Warren County, Mississippi, a daughter of Love Adam Wells and Mary Be. Lanier, both of whom were born in Mississippi. An affidavit made under oath and signed by her sister Amelia Jane Bell of 4575 Aldine, St. Louis, Missouri was accepted as verification of her birth. Supporting evidence consisted of a photostatic copy of the Family Bible record and her St. Louis, Missouri Voter Registration Record #14305 dated 18 October 1967.[22] She died on 15 November 1975 in St. Louis, Missouri. According to her death certificate Jennie J. Lee died at De Paul Hospital in St. Louis from lung cancer at age 65. She had been employed as a switchboard operator at an electrical company in St. Louis and lived at 4323 Enright. Her social security number was listed as 499-05-5545. Jennie was separated from her husband, Jimmie Lee, at the time of her death. She was buried on 19 November 1975 at Washington Park Cemetery. Mable L. Dulaney, her sister from Chicago, gave the information on the death certificate.[23] She married (1) Charles Burrell and they divorced, (2) Mr. Lacy who died, and (3) Jimmy Lee.[24]

x. Liller Wells, born 15 March 1912 in Vicksburg, Mississippi;[25] she died on 17 January 1967 in Chicago, Illinois.[26]

xi. Cleophas Wells, born 18 December 1913 in Vicksburg, Mississippi;[27] died in St. Louis, Missouri. He married Helen Squires in St. Louis.[28]

Conclusion

This first phase of research into the African-American ancestry of Quincy Jones produced a fairly well-documented family group for Love Adam Wells and Mary Bell Lanier while using a limited number of sources. Digging deeper would include obtaining other records to document the lives the children—such as, requesting marriage records to identify spouses and complete marriage entries, searching newspapers for obituary notices that would offer more biographical detail and list their heirs, and studying the arrangement of graves at Washington Park Cemetery to see if any of their spouses or children are buried nearby. Estate records can be searched to find out how their real estate and personal property were distributed after death. Tracking down their descendants who are living today could result in learning more about the daily lives of the Wells children, as well as expanding the current family circle.

---

[1] Marriage Records of Warren County, Mississippi. Colored Marriages, Volume 9, page 437. FHL Film #886062.

[2] 1910 U.S. Census (Population Schedule), Warren County, Mississippi, ED 69, Sheet 5. FHL Film #13744775.

[3] 1900 U.S. Census (Population Schedule) of Beat 4, Warren County, Mississippi, ED 135, Sheet 118A, Line 10. FHL Film #1240831.

[4] State of Missouri Division of Health. Death certificate of Love Wells. State File Number 14768, Registrar's Number 3380. Certified copy in possession of the author.

[5] 1880 U.S. Census (Population Schedule) of Bovina Precinct, Warren County, Mississippi, ED 78, Page 14, Line 25. FHL Film #1254667.

[6] State of Missouri Division of Health. Death certificate of Love Wells, State File Number 14768, Registrar's Number 3380. Certified copy in possession of the author.

[7] *Ibid.*

[8] Marriage Records of Warren County, Mississippi. Colored Marriages, Volume 9, page 437. FHL Film #886062.

[9] State of Missouri Division of Health. Death Certificate of Mary Bell Wells, State File Number 60-040354, Registrar's Number 9994. Certified copy in possession of the author. Amelia J. Bell gave the information on the death certificate. She incorrectly listed Samuel Lenear as the father of the deceased.

[10] *Ibid.*

[11] Family Bible of Love and Mary B. Wells. Photocopy in possession of the author.

[12] *Ibid.*

[13] Family Bible of Love and Mary B. Wells. Photocopy in possession of the author.

[14] *Ibid.*

[15] State of Illinois Coroner's Certificate of Death of Leona Wells, State File Number 631479. Certified copy in possession of the author.

[16] State of Missouri Department of Health. Death certificate of Andrew N. Wells, State File Number 3915, Registrar's Number 0114. Certified copy in possession of the author.

[17] Family Bible of Love and Mary B. Wells. Photocopy in possession of the author.

[18] Month and year of death provided by her son, Quincy D. Jones, Jr.

[19] Mississippi State Board of Health, Division of Vital Statistics. Delayed Certificate of Birth of Armelia Jean Wells filed 12 September 1942.. Certified copy in possession of the author.

[20] State of Missouri Division of Health. Death certificate of Amelia Jean Bell, State File Number 75 202785.

[21] Interview with Mable Dulaney.

[22] Mississippi State Board of Health, Division of Vital Statistics. Delayed Certificate of Birth of Jennie Joyce Wells, filed June 18, 1973.. Certified copy in possession of the author.

23 State of Missouri Division of Health. Death Certificate of Jennie J. Lee, State File Number 124, Registrar's Number 75 208704. Certified copy in possession of the author.

24 Interview with Mable Dulaney.

25 Family Bible record.

26 Interview with Mable Dulaney.

27 Family Bible record.

28 Interview with Mable Dulaney.

Case Study 2
From Nelson to David Wells: Identifying a Former Slave's Owner

Identifying the slave-owning family is a necessary aspect of tracing African American ancestry. There are several ways to do this, depending on the circumstances. Many genealogists begin with the misconception that freed slaves routinely took the name of their last owner. This is not always the case. When newly transported slaves were sold to an American owner, their African identity was replaced with a group identity and a new name. They were given only first names which generally were not duplicated on small farms and plantations. On larger plantations, where duplication did exist, identifying adjectives were appended to names to distinguish one person from another—as, for example, three men on the same plantation were identified in records as Old Dave, Big Dave, and Young Dave.

When the Civil War ended, most former slaves adopted surnames legally. Some slaves had surnames prior to being freed, but many of them kept their choice a secret from the white community. Some slaves changed their names each time they moved to a different plantation and made a final choice after being freed. Once free, others experimented with several surnames before settling on one that suited them. They often took the surname of their father, who may have been a slave on the same plantation, a slave sold to another owner, a deceased slave, a free black, a white neighbor, an overseer, or the slave's owner (who may have been an African-American or Native American himself). The name preferred by a slave may have been that of a current owner, a former owner, a prominent American, a locally prominent citizen, or the given name of the father. A large percentage of former slaves took the surname of the person who owned them at the time of their birth.

After the war former slaves rarely moved further than a few miles from where they lived as slaves. Most went to work as farm laborers for their former owner or the owner's relatives. The most important step in tracing African American ancestry is to identify the owner of a former slave and the plantation where they lived. *Once those two elements are known, research focuses on the owner, his family, and the records they produced that may mention members of a slave family.*

Like many families, the Joneses had recollection of a number of ancestors born into slavery. Quincy's mother, Sarah Frances Wells, who passed away in 1999, remembered her paternal grandfather, Nelson Wells, and maternal grandmother, Cordelia Dickson. Sarah knew that they had been born in Warren County, Mississippi and some family members had worked for the Batchelor family after the war, but she knew nothing of how they made the transition from slavery to freedom or how they acquired a surname.

In the first case study involving this family, proof that Nelson Wells and Sarah Campbell were the parents of Love Adam Wells was found on his death certificate and the family's entry in the 1880 census. Nelson and Sarah had been married only a few years in 1880 and all of their children had not been identified.

Lloyd Jones, the musician's brother, had a note stating that Humphrey Wells was Nelson and Sarah's oldest son and another son, Nelson W. Wells, had on 9 April 1903 (before death records were required in Mississippi). When family members can supply limited or no information about earlier generations, research turns to public records. In this case, marriage and census records filled-in some missing information.

On 18 April 1874, Nelson Wells applied for a marriage license to marry Miss Sarah Campbell. The person who performed the ceremony failed to record the date of their marriage. Normally, people married within a few days of applying for a license.[1] Their entry in the 1900 census follows:[2]

Locality		1900 - Beat 3, Warren County, Mississippi						
ED, Sheet, Line		Enumeration District 138, Page 16, Line 91B						
Enumeration Date		30 June 1900						
Location						Birth Place		
House	Fam.	Name	Birth Date	Relationship	Occupation	Self	Fath	Moth
271	279	Wells, Nelson	Mar 1840	Head	Farmer	MS	MS	MS
		—, Sarah	Nov 1839	Wife		MS	MS	MS
		—, Elder C.	Oct 1881	Son	At School	MS	MS	MS

The census states that they has been married twenty-one years and that Sarah had given birth to three children, of whom only one was living when the census was taken.

Several discrepancies exist between the 1880 and 1900 census entries for Nelson Wells and his family. In 1880, Nelson and Sarah were listed as twenty-six years old and twenty-three years old respectively. If those ages were entered correctly, they should have been forty-six and forty-three years old in 1900. Furthermore, Nelson applied for a marriage license in April 1874 which suggests that they had been married for twenty-six years when the census was taken. Then there's the matter of Nelson W. Wells not appearing with his parents in the 1900 census. Could he have been the Elder C. Wells? The Wells children who were alive in 1983 had never heard of an Uncle Elder Wells. Considering the number of errors in the 1900 enumeration, perhaps Elder C. Wells and Nelson W. Wells are the same person. It is impossible to know for sure how the 1900 census became so riddled with errors, but it appears that an unrelated person gave the information to the enumerator.

Moving back in time, Nelson Wells appears as a child in his father's household on the 1870 census of Warren County, Mississippi—one of the first public records listing the former slaves of that county. The enumeration contains enough information to begin compiling a family group for that generation and an area in which to begin looking for the plantation where they might have lived.[3]

Locality	1870 - Warren County, Mississippi, Bovina Precinct, page 108							
Enumeration Date	21 July 1870							

Location			Descrip.			Value of Estate		Birth	
House	Fam.	Name	Sex	Age	Occupation	Real	Person.	Place	Remarks
840	764	David Wells	M	40	Farm Hand			VM	
		Dorcas "	F	47	"			MS	
		Nelson "	M	18	"			MS	
		Caroline "	F	16	"			MS	
		Gabe "	M	10	"			MS	
		Lucinda "	F	7	"			MS	
		Samuel "	M	3	"			MS	
		Wm. "	M	20	"			MS	
		Sopha "	F	17	"			MS	

This phase of research took place in 1983—before the 1870 census had been indexed. Without an index, records must be searched line-by-line and that approach often produces some interesting surprises. Recalling that Love Adam Wells married Mary Bell Lanier, the daughter James Balance Lanier and Cordelia Dickson, while searching the 1870 census for Nelson Wells, the following entry identified Cordelia's parents:[4]

Locality		1870 - Warren County, Mississippi, Bovina Precinct						
Enumeration Date		21 July 1870						

Location			Description			Value of Estate		Birth	
House	Fam.	Name	Sex	Age	Occupation	Real	Person.	Place	Remarks
840	764	Henry Dickson	M	60	Farm Hand			MD	
		Minerva "	F	38	"			MS	
		Priscilla "	F	22	"			MS	
		Betsy "	F	20	"			MS	
		Cordelia "	F	12	"			MS	
		Rebecca Ransabug	F	25	"			MS	
		Minerva "	F	6	"			MS	
		Victoria "	F	4	"			MS	
		No Name "	F	5mo	"			MS	
		Henry Stocking	M	5mo				MS	

The special slave schedules compiled as part of the 1850 and 1860 census list the name of the slave owner and the sex, age, and color of each slave. None of the slaves is listed by name. No one named Wells or Dickson appears in the slave schedules for either census, which casts doubt on the premise that the Dickson and Wells families took the surname of their last owner.

Sixty-five major landowners (those owning land valued at more than $1,000.00) were living in Bovina Precinct in 1870.[5] David Wells lived closest to Hal P. Noland—who owned a plantation valued at $10,000.00. Hal's immediate neighbor, Ellen Batchelor, owned land valued at $4,000.00. Proving that either of them had owned any or all members of the Wells or Dickson family could lead to discovering earlier generations of their slave ancestry.

Slaves were regarded as the personal property of an owner and as such they could be sold, given, or bequeathed to another person. If an owner died without leaving a will, his or her slaves may have been sold to satisfy the debts of the estate, divided among the heirs of the deceased, or retained by the widow to operate the plantation. The owners of large plantations often wrote lengthy wills explaining how their property should be distributed. Of the two wills written by members of the Noland family and proved in the County Court of Warren County, Mississippi listed slaves as property of the estate.

In the Name of Almighty God, Amen. I Pearce Noland Being weak in body but of sound mind and perfect memory make this my last will and Testament hereby revoking all others made by my hand before; Item 1st, I give and bequeath unto my Son George D. Noland the sum of one hundred Dollars in addition to what I have heretofore given him and his heirs forever. Item 2nd, I give and bequeath to my daughter Eliza [sic] D. Batchelor one hundred Dollars to her and her heirs forever, in addition to what I have heretofore given her. Item 3rd, I give and bequeath to my son [name illegible] one hundred Dollars to him and his heirs forever. Item 4th, I give and bequeath to my son Avery Noland the Sum of one hundred Dollars to him and his heirs forever in addition to what I have heretofore given him. Item 6th, I give and bequeath to my son Pearce Noland one hundred Dollars to him and his heirs forever in addition to what I have heretofore given him. Item 6th, I give and bequeath to my daughter Elizabeth Norwood eight thousand Dollars in cash to be paid by my executor, herein named. Item 7th, I will and bequeath that my Negroes and Stock of every description together with all my personal property on the place I now reside be kept together until all my lawful debts are paid and then I desire that there shall be a division of said property of every description both real and personal and that my wife Elizabeth Noland shall have her dower set apart in the land, Plantation known by the name of Sligo and that my said wife shall have twenty-five Negroes set apart by Families. Item 8th, I then give an bequeath unto my two sons, T. V. Noland and Henry Noland all the balance of said tract of land to be equally divided between them at the time herein before named. The said tract of land lying North of Whites Creek in the Robb Field until it strikes the sectional line between Sections 18 and 19 then West to Markham's line including all the land down in Warren County. Item 9th, I further give and bequeath unto T. V. Noland and Henry Noland my two sons all the balance of my Negroes on said place to be equally divided between them, and it is my desire that three Negroes (to wit): Warren, Sandy, and Jenny shall be allotted to my Son Henry Noland at their appraised value. Item 10th, I give and bequeath to my Son Henry Noland a Negro Boy named Lorenzo who is now learning the Blacksmith Trade. Item 12th, it is my will and desire that all the balance of my property of every description including stock of all Sorts, Farming utensils together with everything else be equally divided between my wife Elizabeth Noland and my two sons T.V. Noland and Henry Noland. Item 13th, I hereby appoint my son T.V. Noland the Sole Executor of my last will and Testament. The 31st day of Jan'y 1857.[6]

Pearce Noland's will, only one of the documents related to his estate, does not mention all of his slaves by name, but it directs that they be divided among his wife and sons, T. V. and Henry Noland. He names Sligo as his plantation and Ellen (the clerk mistakenly wrote Eliza) D. Batchelor as his daughter, which explains the link between the Nolands and the family David Wells worked for after the war.

The Warren County Court held other records associated with the settlement of Pearce Noland's estate. An inventory of his personal property listed slaves in family groups by name, age and value. The aggregate value of his slaves was $98,650—a staggering sum given that a dollar in 1857 would be equal to twenty dollars today .

A Partial List of Slaves Inventoried with the Estate of Pearce Noland			
Description	Name	Age	Value
Negro man	Dixon	40	$1,150
" woman	Manerva	35	500
" boy	Madison	10	700
" girl	Rebecca	13	700
" girl	Lucilla	8	500
" girl	Betsy	6	300
Negro man	Davy	25	$1,300
" woman + child	Dorcas	30	1,500
	unnamed child	5mo	
" girl	Creecy	15	1,000
" boy	Davy Jr.	9	650
" boy	Bill	6	450
" boy	Nelson	5	350

Age discrepancies exist between members of the Wells and Dickson families listed in Pearce Noland's inventory and the 1870 census, but that happened all the time. Sometimes people did not the exact age of a slave and guessed. Rumor that the Federal government would reimburse slave owners if emancipation took place led to fudging on the ages and condition of their slaves. Older slaves became younger and the younger ones aged a year or two. Noland's estate was not divided among his heirs until February, 1862, more than a year after Mississippi had left the Union and four years after his widow had died. The division of property lists 130 slaves, including these two lots:

Final Division of the Estate of Pearce Noland[8]			
Lot 1		Lot 2	
Slave	**Value**	**Slave**	**Value**
Davy Wells	$1,000.00	Henry Dickson	$ 700.00
Dorcas	600.00	Minerva	500.00
Curry	900.00	Rebecca	900.00
Davy Wells, Jr.	750.00	Madison	800.00
Bill	700.00	Priscilla	700.00
Nelson	600.00	Betsy	650.00
Carolina	350.00	Cordelia	225.00
John	200.00	Robert	100.00
Gabe	75.00	Sally	100.00
Jack	150.00		

Having proved that Pearce Noland had owned the Wells and Dickson families as slaves, attention turned to documenting Noland's life to discover how he acquired them, where else they might have lived, and the quality of their lives in Warren County.

Judge Pearce Noland of Sligo Plantation
Pearce Noland, a son of George Noland and Alice Peyton, was born in 1789 in Loudoun County, Virginia. The family migrated to Wilkes County, Georgia where George Noland died in 1800 when Pearce was eleven years old. His other children were William F., Peyton, Avery, Ann and George Noland. On 11 February 1816 in Adams County, Mississippi, Pearce Noland married Elizabeth Ann Galtney, daughter of Abraham Galtney and Nancy Ann Killian.[9]

Pearce is said to have arrived in Mississippi at age thirteen years, probably with his Galtney and Killian relatives. He became the first judge of the county court of Jefferson County, Mississippi in 1820 and continued to serve as a judge after moving to Warren County. No one who has studied Pearce Noland's history disputes the fact that he was educated, wealthy, and respected.

According to the 1860 Census (Slave Schedule) of Warren County, Mississippi, the Noland and Batchelor families owned 240 slaves who lived on three plantations, viz., Sligo, the main plantation where Judge Noland lived with his wife; Gumwood, a smaller plantation, and a third unnamed plantation where John Pearce was the overseer.[10] The Wells and Dickson families lived at Sligo, which is now a cattle ranch.

A few of Pearce Noland's descendants remained in Bovina Precinct as late as 1984. A great-grandson of Hal P. Noland (a son of Pearce Noland), reported that the Noland family lost the plantation to Anderson Tully, who took it over in exchange for the taxes owed on it in the 1930s, but that was after the mansion house burned to the ground around 1900. Pearce Noland's descendants say that if his plantation records and personal diaries survived him, they were destroyed in the fire.

Some slave owners entered the names of their slaves in a special section at the back of their family Bible. The Noland family Bible went to Pearce's son, Hal P. Noland, who passed it on to his daughter Mary Noland Paxton. Family members who have seen the Bible do not recall any entries for their slaves.

A history of St. Alban's Protestant Episcopal Church at Bovina states that "...three weeks after Secession Conference (February 4, 1861) a large number of Negro slaves belonging to the Noland, Batchelor, and Downs families presented themselves at St. Alban's for confirmation by the Bishop."[11] These slaves continued to attend church with white planters and their families and were listed in the parish register as regular communicants. They greatly out-numbered the white membership until St. Alban's became a segregated church at the end of the Civil War.

Pearce Noland founded Oakland College which later became Alcorn A & M, an African American college today. Members of their history department knew very little about the former school and less about Judge Noland.

Having searched widely for personal and public records left by the Noland family in Warren County, Mississippi, the question of when and where he acquired the Wells and Dickson families remains unanswered. Pearce Noland could have inherited some slaves from his father's estate or from the estates of one or more of his grand-parents. The 1870 census shows that David Wells was born in Virginia and Henry Dickson in Maryland. As families migrated from those states they brought their slaves along. The estate records of Pearce Noland's mother and/or grandparents, if found, may list David Wells and Henry Dickson as children. Owners often recorded the Bill of Sale when purchasing a slave. Judge Noland recorded only three such bills of sale with the court in Warren County, but he or members of his family a generation earlier may have recorded others in Adams, Amite or Jefferson County.

It is possible that Pearce Noland purchased David Wells and Henry Dickson from another slave owner. A John Wells lived in Warren County, Mississippi in 1850, but nothing could be found to connect him to Pearce Noland or David Wells. A large group of Wells families lived in Hinds County, which borders Warren County on the east, but again nothing surfaced there that linked to Pearce Noland. Three men named Dixon lived in Warren County, including Roger Dixon whose estate papers were filed there. He owned slaves, but none was named Henry or Minerva.

Conclusion

Tracing and documenting five generations of an African American family takes time, skill, and dedication. Records used to trace slave ancestry can be widely scattered and unindexed. A well-document pedigree from Quincy Jones to David Wells has been compiled, but what about earlier generations? Identifying the parents of David Wells depends on the existence of another estate inventory or final settlement that links him to a family—or possibly some bills of sale proving that he and his parents were sold to Pearce Noland. An even longer shot is finding a complete set of plantation records that list the names, dates of birth, and parents of every slave owned by the planter. A dedicated researcher never gives up. As their skill level increases, they revisit records already searched to see if there's a clue that might have been missed. Even when nothing new surfaces, something new is learned.

---

[1] Marriage Records of Warren County, Mississippi. Colored Marriages, Volume 10, page 278. FHL Film #886063.

[2] 1900 U.S. Census (Population Schedule), Warren County, Mississippi, ED 138, Sheet 16, Line 91B. FHL Film #1240831.

3 1870 U.S. Census (Population Schedule), Warren County, Mississippi, page 108. FHL Film #552250.

4 *Ibid.*

5 *Ibid.* Bovina Precinct.

6 Will Records of Warren County, Mississippi. Will of Pearce Noland. Will Book A, pp. 239-240. FHL Film #879,311.

7 *Ibid.* Inventory of the Property of Pearce Noland, April 1857., pp. 627-632.

8 Probate Records of Warren County, Mississippi. Division of the Estate of Pearce Noland. Minute Book M, 1861-1866. FHL Film 879320.

9 *Biographical and Historical Memoirs of Mississippi.* Chicago: The Goodspeed Publishing Company, 1891, pp. 512-513.

10 1860 U.S. Census (Slave Schedules) of Warren County, Mississippi, pp. 238-241. FHL Film #803603.

11 Marion B. Bragg. *St. Alban's Protestant Episcopal Church.* Vicksburg: Hammer Memorial Library, 1963.

AFRICAN AMERICAN SLAVE NARRATIVES

The following narratives are excerpted from a larger work entitled "Slave Narratives" that is published on CD-ROM and on the Internet by Ancestry.com. For more information on the collection, which contains more than 2,300 narratives from twenty-five states and the District of Columbia, visit <www.ancestry.com>.

ARKANSAS
Clemments, Maria Sutton

I don't know jes how old I is. Yes mim I show do member the war jes lack as if it was yesterday. I was born in Lincoln County, Georgia. My old mistress was named Frances Sutton. She was a real old lady. Her husband was dead. She had two sons Abraham and George. One of them tried to get old missus to sell my ma jes before the war broke out. He wanter sell her cause she too old to bear children. Sell her and buy young woman raise mo children to sell. Put em in the nigger drove and speculate on em. Young nigger, not stunted, strong made, they look at their wristes and ankles and chestes, bout grown bring the owner fifteen hundred dollars. Yes mam every cent of it. Two weeks after baby born see the mother carrin it cross the field fur de old woman what kept all the children and she be going right on wid de hoe all day. When de sun come up the niggers all in the field and workin when de ridin boss come wid de dogs playin long after him. If they didn't chop dat cotton jes right he have em tied up to a stake or a big saplin and beat him till de blood run out the gashes. They come right back and take up whar they left off work. Two chaps make a hand soon as dey get big nuf to chop out a row.

Had plenty to eat; meat, corncake and molasses, peas and garden stuff. They didn't set out no variety fo the niggers. They had pewter bowls to eat outer and spoons. Eat out in the yard, at the cabins, in the kitchen. Kat different places owin to what you be workin at when the bell rung. Big bell on a high post.

My ma's name was Sina Sutton. She come from Virginia in a nigger traders drove when she was sixteen years old and Miss Frances husband bought er. She had nine childen whut lived. I am de youngest. She died jes before de war broke out. Till that time I had been trained a house girl. My ma was a field hand. Then when the men all went to the army I plowed. I plowed four years I recken, till de surrender. Howd I know it was freedom? A strange woman - I never seed fore, come runhin down where we was all at work. She say loud as she could "Hay freedom. You is free." Everything toe out fer de house and soldiers was lined up. Dats whut they come by fer. Course dey was Yankee soldiers settin the colored folks all free. Everybody was gettin up his clothes and leaving. They didn't know whah des goin. Jes scatterin round. I say give 'em somethin. They was so mad cause they was free and leavin and nobody to work the land. The hogs and stock was mostly all done gone then. White folks sho had been rich but all they had was the land. The smoke houses had been stripped and stripped. The cows all been took off cept the scrubs. Folks plowed ox and glad to plow one.

Sometime we had a good time. I danced till I joined the church. We didn't have no nigger churches that I knowed till after freedom. Go to the white folks church. We danced square dance jess like the white folks long time ago. The niggers baptized after the white folks down at the pond. They joined the white folks church sometimes. The same woman on the place sewed for de niggers, made some things for Miss Frances. I recollects that. She knitted and seed about things.

She showed the nigger women how to sow. All the women on the place could card and spin. They set around and do that when too bad weather to be on the ground. They sbow didn't teach them to read. They whoop you if they see you have a book. If they see you gang round talkin, they say they talkin bout freedom or equalization. They scatter you bout.

When they sell you, they take you off. See drove pass the house. Men be ridin wid long whips of cow hide wove together and the dogs. The slaves be walkin, some cryin cause they left their folks. They make em stand in a row sometimes end sometimes they put en up on a high place end auction em.

The pore white folks whut not able to buy hands had to work their own land. There shore was a heap of white folks what had no slaves. Some ob dem say theys glad the niggers got turned loose, maybe they could get them to work for them sometimes and pay em.

When you go to be sold you have to say what they tell you to say. When a man be unruly they sell him to get rid of him heap of times. They call it sellin nigger meat. No use tryin run off they catch you an bring you back. I don't know that there was ever a thought made bout freedom till they was fightin. Said that was what it was about. That was a white mans war cept they stuck a few niggers in front ob the Yankee lines. And some ob the man carried off some man or boy to wait on him. He so used to bein waited on. I ain't takin sides wid neither one of dem I tell you.

If der was anything to be knowed the white folks knowed it. The niggers get passes and visit round on Saturday evening or on Sunday jes mongst theirselves and mongst folks they knowed at the other farms round.

When dat war was done Georgia was jes like being at the bed place. You couldn't stay in the houses fear some Ku Klux come shoot under yo door and bust in wid hatchets. Folks hide out in de woods mostly. If dey hear you talkin they say you talkin bout equalization. They whoop you. You couldn't be settin or standing talkin. They come and ask you what he been tell you. That Ku Klux killed white men too. They say they put em up to hold offices over them. It was heep worse in Georgia after freedom than it was fore. I think the poor nigger have to suffer fo what de white man put on him. Wes had a hard time. Some of em down there in Georgia what didn't get into the cities where they could get victuals and a few regs fo cold weather got so pore out in the woods they nearly starved and died out. I heard em talk bout how they died in piles. Niggers have to have meat to eat or he get weak. White folks didn't have no meat, no flour.

The folks was after some people and I run off and kept goin till I took up with some people. The white folks brought them to Tennessee - Covington - I come too. They come in wagons. My father, he got shot and I never seed him no mo. He lived on another farm fo de war. I lived wid them white folks till bout nine years and I married. My old man wanted to come to dis new country. Heard so much talk how fine it was. Then I had run across my brother. He followed me. One brother was killed in the war somehow. My brother liked Memphis an he stayed there. We come on the train. I never did like no city.

We farmed bout, cleared land. Never got much fo the hard work we done. The white man don learned how to figure the black folks out of what was made cept a bare living.

I could read a little and write. He could too. We went to school a little in Tennessee.

When we got so we not able to work hard he come to town and carpentered, right here, and I cooked fo Mr. Hopkins seven years and fo Mr. Gus Tnweatt and fo Mr. Nick Tnweatt. We got a little ahead then by the hardest. I carried my money right here bag on a string tied around her waist. We bought a house and five acres of land. No mum I don't own it now. We got in hard luck and give a nortgage. They closed us out. Mr. Sanders. They say I can live there long as I lives. But they owns it. My garden fence is down and won't nobody fix it up fo me. They promises to come put the posts in but they won't do it and I ain't able no mo. I had a garden this year. Spoke fo a pig but the man said they all died wid the cholera. So I ain't got no meat to eat dis year.

I ain't never had a chile. I ain't got nobody kin to me livin dat I knows bout. When I gets sick a neighbor woman comes over and looks after me. I thinks if de present generation don't get killed they die cause they too lazy to work. No mum dey don't know nuthin bout work. They ain't got no religion. They so smart they don't pay no tention to what you advise em. I never tries to find out what folks doin and the young generation is killin time. I sho never did vote. I don't believe in it. The women runnin the world now. The old folks ain't got no money an the young ones wastes theirs. Theys able to make it. They don't give the old folks nuthin. The times changes so much I don't know what goiner come next. I jes stop and looks and listens to see if my eyes is foolin me. I can't see, fo de cataracts gettin bad, nohow. Things is heap better now fo de young folks now if they would help dierselves. I'm too wo out. I can't do much like I could when I was young. The white folks don't cheat the niggers outen what they make now bad as they did when I farmed.

I never knowed about uprisings till the Ku Klux sprung up. I never heard bout the Nat Tarner rebellion. I tell you bout the onliest man I knowed come from Virginia. A fellow come in the country bout everybody called Solomon. Dis long fo the war. He was a free man he said. He would go bout mong his color and teach em fo little what they could slip him along. He teached some to read. When freedom he went to Augusta. My brother seed him and said "Solomon, what you doin here?" and he said "I am er teaching school to my own color." Then he said they run him out of

Virginia cause he was learnin his color and he kept going. Some white folks up North learned him to read and cipher. He used a black slate and he had a book he carried around to teach folks with. He was what they called a ginger cake color. They would whoop you if they seed you with booke learnin. Mighty few books to get holt of fo the war. We mark on the ground. The passes bout all the paper I ever seed fo I come to Tennessee. Then I got to go to school a little.

Whah would the niggers get guns and shoot to start a uprisin? Never had none cept if a white man give it to him. When you a slave you don't have nothin cept a big fireplace and plenty land to work.

They cook on the fireplace. Niggers didn't have no guns fo the war an nuthin to shoot in one if he had one whut he picked up somewhere after the war. The Ku Klux done the uprisin. They say they won't let the nigger enjoy freedom. They killed a lot of black folks in Georgia and a few white folks whut they said was in wid em. We darkies had nuthin to do wid freedom. Two or three set down on you, take leaves and build a fire and burn their feet nearly off. That the way the white folks treat the darky.

I never knowed nobody to hold office. Then whut didn't want to starve got someplace whut he could hold a plow hardle. You don't know whut hard times is. Dem was hard times. They used to hide in big cane brakes, nearly wild and nearly starved. Scered to come out. I ain't wanted to go back to Georgia.

I gets the Old Age Pension and meets the wagon and gets a little commodities. I works my garden and raises a few chickens round my house. I trusts in de Lord and try to do right, honey, dat way I lives.

Miller, Hardy

"Mistress, I'll tell you what my mother said. She said she birthed me on Christmas morning in 1852 in sumpter County, Georgia. It was on har old master's place. Γ ¦ght Harring was his name. Old mistress' name was Miss Lizzie. My father belonged to a different owner.

"Mac McClendon and John Mourning was two nigger traders and they brought my mother and sister Nancy and sister Liza and my sister Anna and Hardy Miller—that's me—out here on the train from Americus, Georgia to Memphis and put us on a steamboat and brought us here to Pine Bluff and sold me to Dr. Pope. He was a poor white man and he wanted a pair of niggers. He bought me and Laura Backwith. In them days a doctor examined you and if your heart was sound and your lungs was sound and you didn't have no broken bones—have to pay one hundred dollars for every year you was old. That was in 1862 and I was ten years old so they sold me for one thousand dollars and one thousand dollars for Laura cause she was sound too. Carried us down to Monticello and when I got free my mammy came after me.

"Fore I left Georgia, my daddy belonged to a man named Bill Ramsey. You see niggers used the name of their masters.

"I can remember when I was a boy Bill Ramsey set my father free and give him a free pass and anybody hire him have to pay just like they pay a nigger now. My daddy hired my mammy from her master. My mammy was her master's daughter by a colored woman.

"My daddy had a hoss named Salem and had a cart and he would take me and my mammy and my sister Liza and go to Americus and buy rations for the next week.

"I number when the war started in 1861 my mammy hired me out to Mrs. Brower and she used to git after me and say, 'You better do that good or I'll whip you. My husband gone to war now on account of you niggars and it's a pity you niggers ever been cause he may get killed and I'll never see him again.'

"I member seein' General Bragg's men and General Steele and General Marmaduke. Had a fight down at Mark's Mill. We just lived six miles from there. Seen the Yankees comin' by along the big public road. The Yankees whipped and fought em so strong they didn't have time to bury the dead. We could see the buzzards and carrion cross. I used to hear old mistress say, 'There goes the buzzards, done at all the meat off.' I used to go to mill and we could see the bones. Used to get out and look at their teeth. Mo ma'm, I wasn't scared, the white boys was with me.

"Dr. Pope was good to me, better to me than he was to Master Walter and Master Billy and my young Miss, Anrelis, cause me and Laura was scared of em and we tried to do everything they wanted.

"When the war ended in 1865 we was out in the field gettin' pumpkins. Old master come out and said, 'Hardy, you and Laura is free now. You can stay or you can go and live with somebody else.' We stayed till 1858 and then our mammies come after us. I was seventeen.

"After freedom my mammy sent me to school. Teacher's name was W. H. Young. Name was William Young but he want under the head of W. H. Young.

"I went to school four years and then I got too old. I learned a whole lot. Learned to read and spell and figger. I done pretty good. I learned how to add and multiply and how to cancel and how to work square root.

"What I've been doin' all my life is farmin' down at Fairfield on the Murphy place.

"Vote? Good Lord! I done more votin'. Voted for all the Presidents. Yankees wouldn't let us vote Democrat, had to vote Republican. They'd be there agitatin'. Stand right there and tell me the ones to vote for. I done quit votin'. I voted for Coolidge—we called him College—that's the last votin' I did. One of my friends, Levi Hunter, he was a colored magistrate down at Fairfield.

"Ku Klux? What you talkin' about? Ku Klux come to our house. My sister Ellan's husband went to war on the Yankee side durin' the war—on the Republican side and fought the Democrats.

"After the war the Ku Klux come and got the colored folks what fought and killed em. I saw em kill a nigger right off his mule. Fell off on his sack of corn and the old mule kep' on goin'.

"Ku Klux used to wear big old long robe with bunches of cotton sewed all over it. I member one time we was havin' church and a Kn Klux was hid up in the scaffold. The preacher was readin' the Bible and tellin' the folks there was a man sent from God and say an angel be here directly. Just then the Ku Klux fell down and the niggers all thought 'twas the angel and they got up and flew.

"Ku Klux used to come to the church well and ask for a drink and say, 'I ain't had a bit of water since I fought the battle of Shilch.' "Might as well tell the truth—had just as good a time when I was a slave as when I was free. Had all the hog meat and milk and everything else to eat.

"I member one time when old master wasn't at home the Yankees come and say to old mistress, 'Madam, we is foragin'.' Old mistress say, 'My husband ain't home; I can't let you.' Yankees say, 'Well, we're goin' to anyway.' They say, 'Where you keep your milk and butter?' Old mistress standin' up there, her face as red as blood and say, 'I haven't any milk or butter to spare.' But the Yankees would hunt till they found it.

"After a battle when the dead soldiers was layin' around and didn't have on no uniform cause some of the other soldiers took em, I've heard the old folk what knowed say you could tell the Yankees from the Rebals comse the Yankees had blue veins on their bellies and the Rebels didn't.

"How you want me to tell you bout this young nigger generation? I never thought I'd live to see this young generation come out and do as well as they is doin'. I'm goin' tell you the truth. When I was young, boys and girls used to wear long white shirt come down to their ankles, cause it would shrink, with a hole cut out for their head. I think they is doin' a whole lot better. Got better clothes. Almost look as wall as the white folks. I just say the niggers dressin' better than the white folks used to.

"Then I see some niggers got automobiles. Just been free bout seventy-two years and some of em actin' just like white folks now.

"Well, good-bye—if I don't see you again I'll meet you in Heaven."

COLORADO
Hanner, Moses

"Never lie, work hard, sleep all you can and smoke good tobacco" is the simple philosophy of a long life, by one who has lived to be 93 years old, Moses (Mose) Hanner of Trinidad, Colorado. Part Indian, Spanish and Negro blood flows through the veins of this man who has lived in the State for seventy years. Short in stature, a small piercing eye that is never still, quiet speech, stooped, yet spry for one of his years as he walks, a constant smoker and a lover of the wide open spaces, in brief tells about old Mose, who seldom laughs out, but who has the most pleasing and inviting smile that this writer has witnessed in a long time. On being told that I came all the way from Denver to chat with him, the graciousness of his soul and heart, said "welcome"—hearty welcome in his smile, "sit down and have a pipe-full of good tobacco in my clay pipe that I keep on hands for those who come to see me." Being too polite to refuse, yet somehow I just had a queer feeling as to the many mouths that had touched that old pipe so well aged, however the fear was soon vanished and I was blowing smoke into the air from the strongest pipe that I ever smoked in my life. He informed me that store tobacco was no good—too much dope in it and for that reason he raised his own tobacco along with potatoes, corn and other garden varieties. Once settled under a large cottonwood tree and with the old clay pipe acting as a sort of rock-me-to sleep function, he asked to know "what do you want to know," because he said an old man like him don't know much compared to the city fellers.

However, after a visit of some four hours, with my note book filled to the last page, and my heart thrilled with his stories of venture and the spirit and unseen power that dominates the pioneer, I said: "Why, we City fellers don't know nothing." This old man is the grandest teacher of this day.

As a matter of record he said he thought he was born in Florida, January 1, 1843. His mother was of Indian and Spanish descent and his father came from Jamaica. And, then with a twinkle in his eye, he said "Now don't ask me to prove this, and you have no way to disprove it, because in that day no records were kept of births and deaths of Negroes, and so, throughout the years I have held fast to this fact pertaining to my birth that was told me by my mother, who had to do with the whole transaction."

Living on the Gulf Coast of Florida, his master, a seafaring man and trader, lived with his slaves on the high seas from the everglades of Florida to South America, and so at an early age, with his father, he learned all the arts of sea-going and the manipulation of a pirate ship.

This life was not to his taste, because when he was bad they threatened to feed him to the ever-present sharks who were self-appointed convoys of every vessel that sailed the gulf. He felt that he would not set well in the sharks belly and like Jonah of the Bible, he would be belched up on some unknown shore. And, too, when they left, no one under the sun knew when they would return. Six months, year or years was all one and the same and just another trip. He was [on] one of these cruisers of two years that his mother died, having passed when they had been out to sea for about ten days. On board ship he did all sorts of things, cabin-boy—deck hand—and at times, a dealer of all kinds of misery and pranks to those he dared approach, because a sailor is a tough onion, and he soon became a tough potatoe. As a matter of fact, toughness was the requirement for the first class sea man.

Fighting, gambling, stealing, cheating was a part of the daily routine, without these numbers, the day was dull and without interest. The whale and storm were two things that took the taste out of the mouth of Mose for the life of a sailor. When the storm was on, then it was that he could see ghosts in the form of horses, lions, and other beasts walking on the waves, and of all the noises they would retreat to the hull of the boat and once concealed behind freight and wares of every description he would call for Mamma and cry himself to sleep.

It was during one of these storms that a very kindly man was drawn to the boy and eased his fears by telling of the wonders of the Rockies, Indians and gold running in the streams and creeks, that fish would eat out of your hand, bear, deer, and all kinds of game, the snow and cold weather.

This fired and inspired him, snow! why he had never heard of such a thing. Having heard of Indians, he had one desire, and that was to organize a gang and beat the day lights out of them. Meyers also interested Mose's father in the tales of the West and the joy and inspiration of the father was similar to that of the boy. So much so, that Mose's father resolved when they did land on the lower neck of Southern California he would quit the ship and join the party that Dave Meyers was going to organize to go to Colorado seeking gold. To reach this conclusion was trying for the father, for this had been his lot all his life, and too his fellow sea men would give him the horse laugh every time the matter was mentioned, the very idea of an old sea dog, such as he, after all those years, and now to become a land lobber, it was no more than high treason and should be treated so.

But fate or fortune, whatever you may choose to call it, was against the old man, fever laid its hand on him and demanded a life for a toll and a broken-hearted little boy that watched his father's body given to the waters of the sea as its final resting place.

Dave Meyers comforted the land-loving lad and assured him that he would take the father's place and that life wouldn't be so bad for him in Colorado.

Many months passed before they reached shore and to Mose it was the day of days, the beginning of his new world, but the Captain did see things that way [?] — the boy was just so much money to him and a slave at that. His word was law and order. He questioned the boy about his foolish notion and when he blankly refused to adhere to the captain's demand that he stay with the ship, he was beaten terribly, but it failed to change him, rather it made him more determined, and put the hatred of hell in his heart against the Captain. Hard-boiled deck hands felt for the lad and made it possible for him to escape. He soon located Dave Meyers and joined the party in their overland trip to the Rockies. But this didn't end his troubles. The war was on and young Mose was a slave and with no passport it would be hard for him to go through the many slave states to reach Colorado, so to overcome this Meyers and his company, after picking up two more colored boys, traveled around the Gulf Coast to the West to California and after a year of terrible hardship they landed in what is now known as the Durango Country of the state. Indians, cowboys and the cow country was new to Mose and he said truly this is heaven to the life on the sea. Meyers was true to his promise and was kind to the boy and was a real father. Now 18 years old, school was a dream to Mose, but the kind man Meyers taught him to read and write, as well as to shave and cut hair, and so he soon became a first-class barber and this was his trade until failing eye sight some years ago forced him to retire.

Coming to Denver in 1870 when it was then the mistress of the Rockies he opened a shop on the corner of Larimer near Fifteenth Street and shaved all the big white folks of that day. Among them was the late Senator Teller who was then Governor. The senator was there just to hear him tell these stories.

Cupid shot his arrow at Mose and he fell mortally wounded in the early eighties to the dance hall queen Susie Bell Lane. She died ten years ago.

After serving in the Spanish American War, seeing service in Cuba, he returned to Denver, sold his shop and moved to the then prosperous coke-oven town of Trinidad and here he has lived throughout the years—with a modern home on the edge of town, surrounding this house he has a five acre track and spends his time with old friends raising a garden and playing checkers. He told the writer that he had just returned from the State Fair, where he was displaying his prize winning chickens and hogs, and he boasted of having the best in the Rocky Mountain region and his many blue ribbons vouched safe for the truth of statement. Asked if he was receiving any money to save from the State, his answer was, "No, I saved my money and I can live fairly good. If the big shots don't take it all from me in taxes." Moses has not had a very large association with his own people, yet he is much interested in them and their future. He contends that they all should join the Socialist party, that the hope of the country can only be saved as we put Socialists into office.

DISTRICT OF COLUMBIA
Harris, Mrs. Lancy

I dunno my father nor my mudda. Jessup Powell always went o' Richmond to buy good breeders. Perry Powell (an ex-slave), who died here last month was one o dem da Jessup Powell bought o Richmond. Jessup Powell drawd my father and mudda, den Lewis drawd my father and he took the name o Lewis. Dey neber hab no mo chillen. I didn't no my father. One day my mudda showd me a man driving his missus to town and said dat wus my father.

I remember when he throwd me ma first dress from the hoot of the marriage. I remember whut it look like. Yeah, jes a red dress wid black flowers in it.

Ma bed had fo' posts and a cord running from pos' to pos' to make spring. We sleep in a room wid pot racks near the fire place, a barrel of soap up in a corner, but the floors wus white like a bread tray. Everything wus in one room. We used to call granpa William Joiner cause he wus a black-smith and carpenter. He joined so many things togeder. Ha, ha! my mem'ry goes and comes. Billie was my grandpa's name. My sight is better now than den, wood you blive it?

I didn't work. I used to stay wid Aunt Kate. I done all the cooking for Aunt Kate—ash cake, ho-cake. William Joiner used to fetch possums, coon and sometimes raccoon and rabbit and I used to do the cooking. My husban' and I used to pick cotton every day. When fodder time come I work Sunday. Some Sunday I worked my own garden.

So many chillen didn't wear clothes. But the missus owned the loom and de servants weave. When de chillen are big enough to work dey gib 'em some cloth from the loom. When I got my issue and my clothes wus good I wud make my cloth into dresses and gib to da chillen.

Old man Jessup Powell married the Doctor's wife after the doctor was dead. The doctor had lots o land. All went to his wife so Jessup didn't know how much land he had fo his new missus had plenty o' land and slaves. I reckon dey had well ni 500 or 600 slaves.

Dick Harrison was another slave owner. He was never married, never had no chillen wid the slave girls. He was good to his niggers. He never allowed anybody to whip his slaves. "I neber would for anyone to whip niggers," he wud say. But when Dick need money tho he wud send the nicest looking one to Richmond jail fo sale. (They evidently had no jail on the plantation. The only jail existed was the one in Richmond.)

Old man Henry Downing (nigger-driver) he wud eat you alive—L-o-r-d he wus so mean. Yo' ud better not let him see you wid a book let alone learning to read.

We used to go over to the plantation of ole man Stanley White. Sometimes we used to call him "Stamper." He wud come and preach to us. We wud go up stairs and dey (white folks) downstairs. We had another preacher we used to call Preacher Gold.

I remember Fred Douglass, Perry Coston from Virginia, and a man by the name of Mason. I shook hands with Booker T. Washington.

I joined the church the year Garfield was shot in the 6th depot near the old Center Market.

I have two grandsons living somewhere. Their names are George Barnes and Joseph Dellworth Lee"

KANSAS
Holbert, Clayton

"My name is Clayton Holbert, and I am an ex slave. I am eighty-six years old. I was born and raised in Linn County, Tennessee. My master's name was Pleasant "Ples' Holbert. My master had a fairly large plantation; he had, I imagine, around one hundred slaves."

"I was working the fields during the wind-up of the Civil War. They always had a man in the field to teach the small boys to work, and I was one of the boys. I was learning to plant corn, etc. My father, brother and uncle went to war on the Union side."

"We raised corn, barley, and cotton, and produced all of our living on the plantation. There was no such thing as going to town to buy things. All of our clothing was homespun, our socks were knitted, and everything. We had our looms, and made our own suits, we also had reels, and we carved, spun, and knitted. We always wore yarn socks for winter, which we made. It didn't get cold, in the winter in Tennessee, just a little frost was all. We fixed all of our cotton and wool ourselves."

"For our meat we used to kill fifteen, twenty, or fifty, and sometimes a hundred hogs. We usually had hickory. It was considered the best for smoking meat, when we butchered. Our meat we had then was the finest possible. It had a lot more flavor than that which you get now. If a person ran out of meat, he would go over to his neighbor's house, and borrow or buy meat, we didn't think about going to town.

When we wanted fresh meat we or some of the neighbors would Hill a hog or sheep, and would divide this, and then when we butchered we would give them part of ours. People were more friendly then then they are now. They have almost lost respect for each other. Now if you would give your neighbor something they would never think of paying it back. You could also borrow wheat or whatever you wanted, and you could pay it back whenever you threshed."

"We also made our own sorghum, dried our own fruits. We usually dried all of our things as we never heard of such a thing as canning."

"We always had brandy, wine, and cider on hand, and nothing was thought of it. We used to give it to the children even. When we had corn husks, log rolling, etc., we would invite all of the neighbors over, and then we would serve refreshments of wine, brandy or cider."

"We made our own maple syrup from the maple sugar trees. This is a lot better than the refined sugar people have nowdays, and is good for you too. You can't get this now though, except sometimes and it is awfully high priced. On the plantations the slaves usually had a house of their own for their families. They usually built their houses in a circle, so you didn't have to go out doors hardly to go to the house next to you. If you wanted your house away from the rest of the houses, they could build you a house away from the others and separate."

"I was never sold, I always had just my one master. When slave owners died, if they had no near relatives to inherit their property, they would 'will' the slaves their freedom, instead of giving them to someone also. My grandmother, and my mother were both freed like this, but what they called 'nigger traders' captured them, and two or three others, and they took them just like they would animals. and sold them, that was how 'Ples' Holbert got my mother. My grandmother was sent to Texas. My mother said she wrote and had one letter from my grandmother after that, but she never saw her again."

MINNESOTA
Dorsey, Nelson

Nelson Dorsey is an interesting character. He can be seen shuffling along the halls at the Crispus Attucks Home most any time of the day. His voice has become very soft, his hair quite gray, and his health has begun to fail. He is of medium build and has a dark complexion. He came to St. Paul in 1908 from Arkansas, and was able to support himself up until about eight years ago when he was forced to move to the home for the aged. The farming lands of Minnesota was what attracted Mr. Dorsey to St. Paul.

"I was born in Hines [Hinds] County, Mississippi, on December 3, 1848, and I was about twelve years old when Abraham Lincoln was elected president. Left home and went to Arkansas when I was about twenty-two years old. I married my first wife the first year I came home from the War. We lived together about five years and six months. I married the second time in Arkansas.

"I was in slavery in Hines County and my Master's name was Ackler. We worked all week up to Friday sundown and didn't work any more until the following Monday. My father's name was Louis Dorsey and my mother's was Palina Dorsey. They lived on a plantation at Fort Gibson, Mississippi. When my Master bought my mother, he only owned three slaves, and was running a hotel.

My mother was a fine cook and she did all the cooking in the master's hotel.

"I was in the Civil War for eight months. They came out to our place one October and picked me up and made a soldier out of me. My regiment fought all over the South, but I can remember best when we were fighting in Nashville and around in Tennessee. The last battle we fought was at Richmond, Virginia, or rather we started for Richmond and got as far as Mobile, Alabama, when freedom for the slaves was declared. I went back to my master's plantation after the war and worked on the place for three years. My mother died in 1867 and then I left there, because my father and older brothers didn't treat me right. They took all the money away from me that I made in the three years I worked there after the war, which was about $150.

"When I came home from the war I had $750 coming to me for fighting. I gave all that money to my mother. When I first left, I went to my former mistresses house, and at that time she was living in Vicksburg, Mississippi.

"There were about seventy-five slaves on our plantation. My Master he had several places and my father was in charge of the slaves on all of them. I remember one Christmas Day when I was little my mother was very sick, and the mistress came to our shack and took me up to the big house because my mother was too sick to take care of me. My mistress had a little girl that was just three weeks older than I was, and she raised us together.

"I got married in Old Town Ridge, Arkansas. We lived about a mile from church and we all went every Sunday. We had services in the afternoon, and the white people had services in the morning. A colored man preached most of the time for us.

"The slaves on our plantation jus' had a long row of houses. Some of our beds were made of rope and some of steel. All the plantations had a lot of chickens and corn patches. When the corn was picked we put it in the cribs.

"On Christmas Day we all had fire crackers, and we didn't have to do any work except the necessary chores until after New Year's Day.

"I have never learned how to read and write, but I know everything that's in the Bible from what I was taught about it. I came to St. Paul in 1908, and have lived here ever since. I haven't got any people living that I know about, and have been living here at the Home for a long time."

NORTH CAROLINA
Adams, Louisa

"My name is Louisa Adams. I was bawned in Rockingham, Richmond County, North Carolina. I was eight years old when the Yankees come through. I belonged to Marster Tom A. Covington, Sir. My mother was named Easter, and my father was named Jacob. We were all Covingtons. No Sir, I don't know whur my mother and father come from. Soloman was brother number one, then Luke, Josh, Stephen, Asbury. My sisters were Jane, Frances, Wincy, and I was nex'. I 'members grandmother. She was named Lovie Wall. They brought her here from same place. My aunts were named, one was named Nicey, and one was named Jane. I picked feed for the white folks. They sent many of the chillun to work at the salt mines, where we went to git salt. My brother Soloman was sent to the salt mines. Luke looked atter the sheep. He knocked down china berries for 'em. (Dad and mammie had their own gardens and hogs. We were compelled to walk about at night to live. We were so hongry we were bound to steal or parish. This trait seems to be handed down from slavery days. Sometimes I thinks dis might be so.) Our food was bad. Marster worked us hard and gave us nuthin. We had to use what we made in the garden to eat. We also et our hogs. Our clothes were bad, and beds were sorry. (We went barefooted in a way. What I mean by that is, that we had shoes part of the time. We got one pair o' shoes a year. When dey wored out we went barefooted. Sometimes we tied them up with strings, and they were so ragged de tracks looked like bird tracks, where we walked in the road. We lived in log houses daubed with mud. They called 'em the slaves houses. My old daddy partly raised his chilluns on game. He caught rabbits, coons, an' possums. He would work all day and hunt at night. We had no holidays. They did not give us any fun as I know. I could eat anything I could git. I tell you de truth, slave time was slave time wid us. My brother wore his shoes out, and had none all thu winter. His feet cracked open and bled so bad you could track him by the blood. When the Yankees come through, he got shoes.)

"I was married in Rockingham. I don't 'member when. Mr. Jimmie Covington, a preacher, a white man, married us. I married James Adams who lived on a plantation near Rockingham. I had a nice blue wedding dress. My husband was dressed in kinder light clothes, best I rickerlect. It's been a good long time, since den tho.

"I sho do 'member my Marster Tom Covington and his wife too, Emma. De old man was the very nick. He would take what we made and lowance us, dat is lowance it out to my daddy after he had made it. My father went to Steven Covington, Marster Tom's brother, and told him about it, and his brother Stephen made him gib father his meat back to us. "My missus was kind to me, but Mars. Tom was the buger. It was a mighty bit plantation. I don't know how many slaves was on it, there were a lot of dem do'. Dere were overseers two of 'em. One was named Bob Covington and the other Charles Covington. They were colored men. I rode with them. I rode wid 'em in the carriage sometimes. De carriage had seats dat folded up. Bob was overseer in de field, and Charles was carriage driver. All de plantation was fenced in, dat is all de fields, wid rails; de rails was ten feet long. We drawed water wid a sweep and pail. De well was in the yard. De mules for the slaves was in town, dere were none on the plantation. Dey had 'em in town; dey waked us time de chicken crowed, and we went to work just as soon as we could see how to make a lick wid a hoe.

"'Lawd, you better not be caught wid a book in yor han'. If you did, you were sold. Dey didn't 'low dat. I kin read a little, but I can't write. I went to school after slavery and learned to read. We didn't go to school but three or four week a year, and learned to read.

"Dere was no church on the plantation, and we were not lowed to have prayer meetings. No parties, no candy pullings, nor dances, no Sir, not a bit. I 'member goin' one time to the white folkses church, no baptizing dat I 'member. Lawd have mercy, ha! ha! No. De pateroller were on de place at night. You couldn't travel without a pas.

"We got few possums. I have greased my daddy's beck after he had been whupped until his back was cut to pieces. He had to work jis the same. When we went to our houses at night, we cooked our suppers at night, et s and then went to bed. If fire was out or any work needed doin' around de house we had to work on Sundays. They did not gib us Christmas or any other holidays. We had corn shuckings. I herd 'em talkin' of cuttin de corn pile right square in two. One wud git on one side, another on the other side and see which out beat. They had brandy at the corn shuckin' and I herd Sam talkin' about gittin' drunk.

"I 'member one 'oman dying. Her name was Caroline Covington. I didn't go to the grave. But you know they had a little cart used with hosses to carry her to the grave, Jist a one horse wagon, jist slipped her in there.

"Yes, I 'member a field song. It was 'Ch! come let us go where pleasure never dies. Great fountain gone over. Dats one uv 'em. We had a good doctor when we got wick. He come to see us. The slaves took herbs dey found in de woods. Dats what I do now, Sir. I got some 'erbs right in my kitchen now.

"When the Yankees come through I did not know anything about 'em till they got there. Jist like they were poppin up out of de ground. One of the slaves was at his master's house you know, and he said, 'The Yankees are in Cheraw, S?? ?? and the Yankees are in town'. It didn't sturb me at tall. I was not afraid of de Yankees. I 'member dey went to Miss Emma's house, and went in de smoke house and emptied every barrel of lasses right in de floor and scattered de cracklings on de floor. I went dere and got some of 'em. Miss Emma was my missus. Dey just killed de chickens, hogs too, and old Jeff the dog; they shot him through the thoat. I 'member how his mouth flew open when dey shot him. One ?? 'em went into de tater bank, and we chillun wanted to go out dere. Mother wouldn't let us. She was fraid uv 'em.

"Abraham Lincoln freed us by the help of the Lawd, by his help. Slavery was owin to who you were with. If you were with some one who was good and had some feelin's for you it did tolerable well; yea, tollerable well.

"We left the plantation soon as de surrender. We left' right off. We went to goin' towards Fayetteville, North Carolina. We climbed over fences and were just broke down chillun, feet sore. We had a little meat, corn meal, a tray, and mammy had a tin pan. One night we came to a old house; some one had put wheat straw in it. We staid there, next mornin', we come back home. Not to Marster's, but to a white 'oman named Peggy McClinton, on her plantation. We stayed there a long time. De Yankees took everything dey could, but dey didn't give us anything to eat. Dey give some of de 'omen shoes.

"I thinks Mr. Roosevelt is a fine man and he do all he can for us.

OREGON
Southworth, Lou

"Lou Southworth was born a slave in Kentucky, was taken to Missouri, and then brought to Oregon as a slave in 1851. He purchased his freedom in Oregon with gold which he dug out of the Yerka and Jacksonville mines. He fought in the Rouge River Indian War, in which he was wounded. Subsequently he built a home and married. He became widely known for his hospitality and public spirit, and his happiness would have been complete but for one circumstance - his white brethren dropped his name from the church roll for playing the violin. This weighed heavily unpon his mind, and in later years, he expressed his feelings as follows:

"'The brethren wouldn't stand for my violin, which was all the company I had most of the time. They said it was full of all sorts of wicked things and that it belonged to the devil. And it hurt me a good deal when they told me that playin' a fiddle is a proceedin' unbecomin' to a Christian in the sight of the Lord. So I told them to keep me in the church with the fiddle if they could, but to turn me out if they must, for I couldn't think of parting with my old-time friend. They turned me out and I reckon my name isn't written in their books here any longer, but I somehow hope it is written in the Big Book up yonder in the land of golden harps where they arent so particular about the old man's fiddle.'

"'And I know, friends, you won't think hard of me and give me the cold shoulder for loving my fiddle these many years. I sometimes think that when you go upyonder and find my name to your surprise in the Big Book, you'll meet many a fellow who remembers the old fiddler who played 'Home Sweet Home,' "Dixie Land,' 'Arkansas Traveler,' 'Swanee River,' and other tunes for the boys who were far away from home for the first time. And some of the fellows will tell how the poor, homesick boys listened to the fiddle during the long winter evenings until they forgot their troubles so they could sleep as they had slept under their mothers' roofs at home. And they'll talk over the days when there was no society for men like us out West: when there wasn't any Bible, and hymn books were unknown, when playin' poker and buckin' faro were the only schoolin' a fellow ever got; when whiskey ran like water and made the whites and Indians crazy; when men didn't go by their right names and didn't care what they did, and when there no law and the court was the man who car-ried the best sixshooter. And when they have talked over those early days, the fellows will say:

"'Where'd we all been and what'd we all done in the mines, but for Uncle Lou's fiddle, which was the most like church of anything we had? For the boys used to think the good Lord put a heap of old-time religious music into my fiddle; and the old-time religious music is good enough for the old man who's done some mighty hard work in eighty-five years.'

"'But I forgot the work I've done and the years I've lived when my bow comes down soft and gentle-like and the fiddle seems to sing the songs of slavery days till the air grows mellow with music and the old-time feelin' comes back, and I can hear familiar voices that are no more.

"'There are things a plain old man can't tell in words, and there are feelin's that won't fit into common everyday talk like mine. When there's plenty of rosin on the bow and the player feelin' fine, and the fiddle pours out great torrents of music that calm down till he hears the bob white's whistle and the rustlin' of the corn, and the whippoorwill and mockin' bird come to sing for him, and he forgets what he ought not to remember and he wants to make everybody glad - then it is that a plain man has feelin's he can't describe. But he knows he's happier and better, and his next day's work is easier. He has a smile and a kind word for every one he meets, and every one has a smile and a kind word for him. The world is heavenly to that man, and his feelin's are nigh on to religious..."'

RHODE ISLAND
Johnson, Henry

Henry Johnson was born in Richmond, Virginia, December 25, 1834. His parents, George Washington and Christina Johnson, were slaves under a man named Thomas Johnson, from whom they received their names. (It was the custom in those days for slaves to take the family name of their master). Henry says that his master and family were very kind to their slaves, "of which he had over 700." Some of the other slave owners were not so good.

Mr. Johnson (the master) bought, but did not sell his slaves (because he did not want them to be ill treated). He used them on his plantation for work around the house, and barns and in the fields where he grew corn, oats, wheat, cotton, tobacco, as well as table vegetables. Some of the slaves made cloth of cotton as well as wool from the sheep on the plantation. The plantation was self sustaining.

Henry Johnson claims that his master would not allow any of his slaves to do any heavy work until they were twenty-one years old (the younger children were not allowed to anything outside of the light chores around the plantation until they were fourteen years old) for fear that they would be stunted and not be able to give a good day's work when they were older. They were not given any schooling because the master wanted to keep them ignorant—if they learned too much they were liable to run away.

After he was twenty-one years old Mr. Johnson was put to work around the plantation, cutting wheat with a scythe—that is, cutting it from places where the machines (wheat reapers) could not go. He drove horses, hauling wood, chopped down trees and cut them into cord wood, cultivated the garden and did all other types of farm work.

The slaves on the Johnson plantation lived in their own houses which were furnished by the master. The furniture was plain but substantial, and consisted of beds, a cook stove, chairs and a couch. Each family had its own separate house in which it did its own cooking, the food being furnished by their master.

There was only one holiday a year for the Johnson slaves and that was on Christmas day. On that day no one worked except the four servants who looked after the master's home. The holiday was celebrated by feasting, the meal being better than the every day ration. On that day they were given fresh meat (chicken or pork) instead of the salted meat which was supplied on other days.

Some of the slaves of the various slave families would get together on that day and sing songs and play games, while others would take advantage of the respite of doing nothing.

The slaves were not allowed off of the plantation to mix with the slaves from other plantations. They were never given money. In fact, many didn't even know what it was, and wouldn't know what to do with it if they had it.

When the Civil War broke out Mr. Johnson was the slave who saddled his master's horse when the master went to enter the army as a lieutenant on the side of the Rebels. He was wounded in the leg and came home for two weeks while the wound healed.

When the war was over Mr. Johnson told all of his slaves that they were free to go where they pleased or they could stay and work for him at their regular work for which he would pay them at the rate of one dollar a day and board. Most of them stayed, for they had no other place to go. Others left him, wandering around trying to find work, and as Henry says "I bet they were back before long."

He stayed with the master for five years after the war, then decided to try out for himself. He found work with the Millen Iron Foundry of Richmond, Va., wheeling coal to the furnace, for which he was paid $1.80 a day. He worked there for one year when a man came down from New York and picked out forty-eight employees from the foundry to work for the New York Water Water Works Co., piping the Tarrytown tunnel. Mr. Johnson was one of the men picked. When they arrived in New York they found that there was a strike on. On finding this condition they refused to work until the strike was settled. (Mr. Johnson says, "I didn't want to get my head knocked off.") When the strike was settled they were put to work, the transportation cost being taken from their wages. Mr. Johnson worked as a steam driver. After this job was finished he went to sea for two years working as a cook and then returned to his old occupation working for various water works in different cities and towns until he finally settled here in Burrillville, where he has lived for a good many years.

In the olden days a ship would sail into the harbor at Key West, Africa on the pretense of buying a load of Guano (bird manure) which was loaded by Negro men and women who worked for a day's pay, when the ship was loaded the officers would give the signal and the boat would pull out without warning, thereby trapping the colored people who were unable to get to shore. They were then brought to America and sold on the "Auction Block" to the highest bidder, a young man or woman about the age of twenty-five would bring about $2,000. It was on one of these trips that the parents of Mr. Johnson were trapped.

In spite of his years Mr. Johnson has a few gray hairs, most of his natural teeth and is able to cut cord wood and enjoy life in a way which astonishes younger folks.

He walks to Pascoag, a distance of four miles, and back three or four times throughout the year. When asked to what he attributed his long life, Mr. Johnson answered, "If you want to live to a ripe old age, take plenty of exercise, walk instead of ride where you wish to go, at least three or five miles a day; walk moderate, don't hustle, eat until you are full, when eating meat don't throw the fat away; the grease keeps your lungs and muscles in good trim. Do this and you will never need a doctor." Mr. Johnson says that he has never been to a doctor or a barber, he does not believe in perfumed soaps atc. He uses tar soap even when shaving.

When we left, Mr. Johnson was giving us a display of his skill with the ax.

VIRGINIA
Berry, Fannie
Nat Turner

Back 'fore the sixties, I can 'member my Mistress, Miss Sara Ann, comin' to de window an' hollerin', "De niggers is arisin'! De niggers is arisin'! De niggers is killin' all de white folks, killin' all de babies in de cradle!" It must have been Kat Turner's Insurrections which was sometime 'fo de breakin' of de Civil War.

I was waitin' on table in dinin' room an' dis day dey had finished eatin' early an' I was cleanin' off table. Don't you know I must have been a good size gal.

John Brown

Yes, I 'member something 'bout him too. I know my Master same home an' said, dat on his way to de gallows ole John stopped an' kissed a little nigger child. "How son' I don't 'member? Don't tell me I don't 'cause I do. I don't care if its done bin a thousand years." I know what Master said an' it is as fresh in my mind as it was dat day. Dis is de song I herd my Master sings:

> Old John Brown came to Harpers Ferry Town,
> Purpose to raise an insurrection;
> Old Governor Wise put the speaks upon his eyes
> An' showed him the happy land of Canaan.

Invention

My Master tole us dat de niggers started the railroad, an' dat a nigger lookin' at a boilin' coffee pot on a stove one day got the idea dat he could cause it to run by putting wheels on it. Dis nigger being a blacksmith put his thoughts into action by makin' wheels an' put coffee on it, an' by some kinder means he made it run an' the idea was stole from him an' day built de steam engine.

Relationship

I was one slave dat de poor white man had his match. See Miss Suel Dese here ol' white men said, "what I can't do by fair means I'll do by foul." One tried to throw me but he couldn't. We tasseled an' knocked over chairs an' when I got a grip I scratched his face all to pieces; an dar was no more bothering Funnie from him; but oh, honey, some slaves would be beat up so, when dey resisted, an' sometimes if you'll 'bolled de overseer would kill yo'. Us Colored women had to go through a plenty, I tell you.

Marriage

Elder Williams married me in Miss Delia Mann's (white) parlor on de crater road. The house still stands. The house was full of Colored people. Miss Sue Jones an' Miss Molley Clark (white), waited on me. Day took de

lamps an' we walked up to de preacher. One waiter joined my han' an' one
my husband's han'. After marriage de white folks give me a 'ception; an',
honey, talkin' 'bout a table—hit was stretched clean 'cross de dinin' room.
We had everythin' to eat you could call for. Me, didn't have no common
eats. We could sing in dar, an' dance ol' squar' dance all us choosed,
ha!ha!ha!Lord! Lord! I can see dem gals now on dat flo', jes skippin' an' a
trottin'. An' honey, dar was no white folks to set down an' eat 'fo you.

Song

> *Kimo, Kimo, dar you are*
> *Hoh, ho rump to pume did'dle.*
> *Set back pinkey wink,*
> *Come Tom Nippceat*
> *Sing song Kitty cat, can't*
> *You carry me o'ert*
> *Up de darkies head so bold*
> *Sing song, Kitty, can't you*
> *Carry me O'or?*
> *Sing Song, Kitty, can't yo'*
> *Carry me home?*

I was at Pamelin an' de Yankees an' Rebels were fightin' an' day were
wavin' the bloody flag an' a confederate soldier was upon a post an' they
wore shootin' terribly. Guns were firin' everywhere.

All a sudden dey struck up Yankee Doodle Song. A soldier dame along and
called to me, "Now far is it to the Rebels", an I honey, was feered to tell hims
So, I said, "I don't know". He called me again. Scared to death I was. I recollect gittin' behind the house an' pointed in the direction. You ace, of de Rebels
knew dat I told the soldier, they would have killed me. These were the Union
men goin' after Lee's army which had don' bin 'fore dem to Appomattox.

The Colored regiment came up behind an' when they saw the Colored
regiment they put up the white flag. (Yo' 'member 'fo' dis red or bloody
flag was up). Now, do you know why dey raised dat white flag! Well,
honey, dat white flag was a token dat Los, had surrendered.

Glory! Glory! yes, child the Negroes are free, an' when they knew dat
dey were free dey, Oh! Baby! began to sing:

> *Many don't yo' cook no mo',*
> *Yo' ar' free, yo' ar' free.*

Rooster don't yo' crow no, mo',
Yo' ar' free, yo' ar' free.
Ol' hen, don't yo' lay no no' eggs,
Yo' free, yo' free.

Sech rejoicing an' shout In', you never he'rd in you' life.

Yes, I can recollect de blowin' up of the Crater. We had fled, but I do know 'bout the shellin' of Petersburg. We left Petersburg when de shellin' commenced an' went to Pamplin in box cars, gettin' out of de way. Dem were seared times too, cause you looked to be kilt any minute by stray bullets. Just before the shollin' of Petersburg, dey were sellin' niggers for little nothin' hardly.

Junius Broadie, a white man bought some niggers, but dey didn't stay slave long, cause de Yankees came an' set 'em free.

Crawley, Charles

God Knows how old I am, All I know is I was born 'fore de war. Yes, I was a slave an' belonged to a family of Allen's in Luenburg County, came here to dis Petersburg de second week of Lee's surrender.

My Marster and Fistese was good to we as well as all us slaves. Day owned 'bout fifty head of Colored People. All de work I did was to play an' drive cows, being only a boy worked around as chillun; doin' dis, an' dat, little things de white folks would call me to do.

Marster Allen, owned my Mother, an' sister too; we emigrant (emigrated) here, came to dis town of Petersburg after Lee's surrender, I mean you now de ending of de Civil War. My mother, sister, and I came on down de road in a box car, which stopped outside de outskirts; hit didn't go through de city. Yes, I know when de first railroads were built, de Norfolk and Western an' de Atlantis Coast Line dey were run through Petersburg an' in dem days it was called de Southern.

Mis and Mars' Allen didn't want us to leave dat part of de Country to come to dis here place down de road, but we comed ourselves to make a home fo' ourselves. Well now, we worked here an' dar, wid dis here man an' dat man; O well, wid different people 'til we bought us selves a home an' paid for it. Mother died right here in dis here house; twelve years age, dis comin' March 'leventh. I am yet livin' in dis same house, dat she an' us all labored as' worked fo' by de sweat of our brow, an' wid dese hard, Lord! Lord! Child dem days was some days. Lemme finish, baby, tellin' you 'bout dis house. De groun' was bought from a lady (Colored) name Sis Jackey, an' she was sometimes called in dem days de Mother of Harrison Street Baptis' Church. I reckon dis church is de ol'est one in Petersburg.

O, yes, honey, I can 'number when de Yankees came into dis town! day broke in stores an' told all do niggers to go in an' git enything dey wanted.

When slaves ran away they were brought back to their Master and Mistess; when dey couldn't catch 'em they didn't bother, but let 'em go. Sometimes do slaves would go an' take up an' live at tother places; some of 'em lived in de woods off of takin' things, sech as hogs, corn, an' vegetables from other folks farm. Well, if dose slaves was caught, dey were sold by their New masters to go down South. Day tell me dem Masters down South was so mean to slaves day would let 'em work dem cotton fields 'til dey fall dead wid hoes in dare hands, 'em would beat dem. I'm glad to say we had good owners.

There was a auction block, I saw right here in Petersburg on the corner of Sycamore street and Bank street. Slaves were auctioned off to de highest bidder. Some refused to be sold by dat I mean, "cried". Lord! Lord! I dons seen dem young 'uns fout and kick like crazy folks child it was, pitiful to see 'em. Dem dey would handcuff an' beat 'em unmerciful. I don' like to talk 'bout back dar. It brin' a sad feelin' up me. If slaves 'belled, I done seed dem whip 'em wid a strop sal' "eat mine tails." Honey, dis strop was 'bout bread as yo' hand, from thum' to little finger, an' 'twas out in strips up. Yo' done seen dese whips dat they whip horses wid? Well dey was used too.

You sed somethin' 'bout how we served God. Um, um, child, I tell you jest how we use to do. We use to worship at different houses. You see you would git a remit to go to dese places. You would have to show your remit. If de Pattyrollers, caught you dey would whip yo'. Date de wa' dey done in dem da's. Pattyrollers, is a gang of white men gitting together goin' through de country catching slaves, an' whipping am' beatin' 'em up if dey had no remit. Marster Allen wouldn't 'llow no one to whip an' beat his slaves, an' he would handle anybody if dey did; so, Marster's slaves met an' worshipped from house to house, an honey, we talked to My God all us wanted.

You know we use to call Marster Allen, Colonel Allen. His name was Robert. He was a home general, an' a lawyer, too. When he went to court any slave he said to free, was freed an' turned aloose. De white fo'ks as well as slaves obeyed Marster Allen.

Did you know poor whites like slaves had to git a pass? I mean, a remit like as slaves, to sell anythin' an' to go places, or de anythin'. Jest as we Colored People, dey had to go to some big white man like Colonel Allen, dey did. If Marster wanted to, he would give des a remit or pass, an' if he didn't feel like it, he wouldn't do it. It was jes as he felt 'bout hit. Date what made all feared him. Ol' Marster was more hard on dem poor white folks den he was on us niggers.

I don't know but two sets of white falks slaves up my way! One was name Chatman, an' de tother one Mellovies. Dese two families worked on Allen's farm as we did. Off from us on a plot called Morgan's let, there day lived as slaves jes like us Colored fo'ks. Yes do poor white man had some dark an' tough days, like us poor niggers! I mean were lashed an' treated, some of 'em, jes as pitiful an' unmerciful. Lord! Lord! baby, I hope yo' young fo'ks will never know what slavery is, an' will never suffer as yo' fore parents. O God: God: I'm livin' to tell de tale to yo', honey. Yes, Jesus, you've spared me.

For clothin' we wore 'loved two suits a year—one for spring, am' one for winter, was all yo' had. De underclothes were made at home. Yo' also got two pairs of shoes an' hats an' capt. The white folks or your slave own-ers would teach dem who could catch on easy an' dey would teach de other slaves, an' dats how dey kept all slaves clothed. Our summer hate wore made out of plaited straw, underclothes made out of sacks an' bags.
We had plenty of feed sech as 'twas cornbread, butter milk, sweet potatoes, in week days. Ha ! Ha ! honey, guess dats why niggers don't like cornbread today! dey got a dislike for dat bread from back folks. On Sunday we had biscuits, and sometimes a little extra food, which old Mistess would send out to Mother for us.

For as I think, if slavery had lasted, it would have been pretty tough. As it was, some fared good, while others fared common. You know, slaves who were beat an' treated bad; some of dem had started gittin' together an' killin' de white folks when day carried dem out to de field to work. God is punishin' some of dem ol' suckers an' their chillun right now for de way day use to treat us poor colored fo'ks.

I think by Negro gittin' educated he has profited, an' dis here younger generation is gwine to take nothin' off dese here poor white folks when day don't treat dem right, cause now dis country is a free country!

ADDITIONAL AFRICAN AMERICAN SOURCES

Following is a collection of African American resources taken from a publication entitled "Afro-American Family History at the Newberry Library" by David Thackery. For current locations and microfilm numbers consult your librarian.

GENERAL SOURCES

Guides and Tools for Genealogical research

Cerny Johni and Arlene Eakle. *Ancestry's Guide to Research: Case Studies in American Genealogy*. Salt Lake City, Utah: Ancestry, 1985.

Crandall, Ralph. *Shaking Your Family Tree: A Basic Guide to Tracing You Family's Genealogy*. Dublin, N. H.: Yankee, 1986.

Doane, Gilbert H. and James B. Bell. *Searching for Your Ancestors: The How and Why of Genealogy*. Minneapolis, Minn.: Univ. of Minnesota, 1980.

Eichholz, Alice, ed. *Ancestry's Red Book: American State, County & Town Sources. Revised edition*. Salt Lake City, Utah: Ancestry, 1992.

Everton, George B. *The Handy Book for Genealogists (8th edition)*. Logan, Utah: Everton, 1991.

Greenwood, Val D. *The Researcher's Guide to American Genealogy (3rd edition)*. Baltimore, Md.: Genealogical Publishing Co., 2000.

Kemp, Thomas. *The International Vital Records Handbook*. Baltimore, Md.: Genealogical Publishing Co., 1990.

Guides and Bibliographies for African American Genealogy

Black Studies: A Select Catalog of National Archives Microfilm Publications. Washington, D.C.: National Archives, 1984.

Blockson, Charles with Ron Fry. *Black Genealogy.* Englewood Cliffs, N.J.: Prentice-Hall, 1977.

Lawson, Sandra M. *Generations Past: A Selected list of Sources for Afro-American Genealogical Research.* Washington, D.C.: Library of Congress, 1998.

Rose, James and Alice Eichholz. *Black Genesis.* Detroit, Mich.: Gale, 1978.

Streets, David H. *Slave Genealogy: A Research Guide with Case Studies.* Bowie, Md.: Heritage, 1986.

Thackery, David T. and Dee Woodtor. *Case Studies in Afro-American Genealogy.* Chicago, Ill.: The Newberry Library, 1989.

Walker, James D. *Black Genealogy: How to Begin.* Athens, Ga: University of Georgia, 1977.

Young, Tommie Morton. *Afro-American Genealogy Sourcebook.* New York, N.Y.: Garland, 1987.

Biographical Compendia

Logan, Rayford W. and Michael R. Winston. *Dictionary of American Negro Biography.* New York, N.Y.: W.W. Norton, 1982.

Mott, Alexander. *Biographical Sketches and Interesting Anecdotes of Persons of Color.* New York, N.Y.: M. Day, 1839.

Simmons, William J. *Men of Mark: Eminent, Progressive and Rising.* Cleveland, Ohio: G.M. Rewell & Co., 1887.

Who's Who of the Colored Race: A General Biographical Dictionary of Men and Women of African Descent: Volume One- 1915. Detroit, Mich.: Gale, 1976 (reprint).

Manuscript Sources and Guides

1. General

National Union Catalog of Manuscript Collections. Washington, D.C.: Library of Congress, 1959-. A valuable aid in determining the location of plantation or other records of slave owning families. Rendered easier for consultation by the publication of the two volume Index to Personal Names... 1959-1984.

Stampp, Kenneth M. ed. *Records of Ante-Bellum Southern Plantations from the Revolution through the Civil War.* Frederick, Md.: University Publications of America, 1985-. Includes many slave records.

2. Guides to Individual Collections

Cain, Barbara T. *Guide to Private Manuscript Collections in the North Carolina State Archives.* 3rd revised edition. Raleigh, N.C.: N.C. Division of Archives and History, 1981.

Cook, D. Louise. *Guide to the Manuscript Collections of the Atlanta Historical Society.* Atlanta, Ga.: The Society, 1976.

Cox, Richard J. and Larry E. Sullivan. *Guide to the Research Collections of the Maryland Historical Society.* Baltimore, Md.: The Society, 1981.

Guide to the Manuscript Collections in the Duke University Library. Santa Barbara, California: ABC-CLIO, 1980.

Guide to the Manuscript Collections of the Virginia Historical Society. Richmond, Va.: The Society, 1985.

Guide to the Microfilmed Manuscript Holdings of the Tennessee State Library and Archives. [Nashville, Tenn.]: The Library and Archives, 1983.

Plunckett, Michael. *A Guide to the Collections Relating to Afro-American History, Literature & Culture in the Manuscripts Department of the University of Virginia Library*. Charlottesville, Va: U. of Va., 1990.

Stokes, Allen H., Jr. *A guide to the Manuscript Collection of the South Caroliniana Library*. Charlottesville, Va.: U. of Va., 1990.

Trimble, Jeanne Slater. *Guide to Selected Manuscripts Housed in the Division of Special Collections and Archives*, Margaret I. King Library, University of Kentucky. [Louisville, Ky.]: U of Ky., 1987.

African Methodist Episcopal Church

Tanner, Benjamin T. *An Apology for African Methodism*. Baltimore: 1867. Contains relatively extensive biographical sketches of church leaders.

Walls, William, J. *The African Methodist Episcopal Zion Church: Reality of the Black Church*. Charlotte, N.C.: A.M.E. Zion, 1974.

Wayman, Alexander W. *Cyclopaedia of African Methodism*. Baltimore: Methodist Episcopal Book Depository, 1882. Contains brief biographical sketches of preachers, deacons and lay leaders throughout the United States.

Periodicals

Journal of the Afro-American Historical and Genealogical Society. Many of the more substantial pieces from this valuable quarterly journal are listed in this bibliography under the appropriate individual headings. Also see: Walker, Barbara. *Index to the Journal of the Afro-American Historical and Genealogical Society: Issues of 1980-1990*. Bowie, Md.: Heritage, 1991.

Southern Workman and Hampton Record (1872-1939). The Hampton Normal School played an important role in African American education, one aspect being the training of black educators who were to find teaching positions throughout the country.

Liberia

Brown, Robert T. *Immigrants to Liberia 1843 to 1904: An Alphabetical Listing.* Philadelphia: Institute for Liberian Studies, 1980. Age and state of origin among the data listed. Some of these emigrants returned to the Unites States.

Murdza, Peter J. Jr. *Immigrants to Liberia 1865 to 1904: An Alphabetical Listing.* Philadelphia: Liberian Studies Association, 1975. Age, family relationships and United States residence among the data listed. Some of these emigrants returned to the United States.

Schick, Tom W. *Emigrants to Liberia 1820-1843: An Alphabetical Listing.* Newark, Del.: Liberian Studies Association, 1971. Age and state of origin among the data provided. Some of these emigrants returned to the United States.

Serial Set 28th Congress 2nd Session (Senate), Volume 9. Contains 1843 Liberian census, as well as roll of emigrants to September 1843.

Stewart, Roma Jones. *Liberia Genealogical Research.* Chicago: Homeland Publications, 1991.

Slave Narratives

1. Compendia

Blassingame, John W. ed. *Slave Testimony: Two Centuries of Letters, Speeches, Interviews, and Autobiographies.* Baton Rouge, La.: Louisiana University Press, 1977.

Rawick, George P. ed. *The American Slave: A Composite Autobiography*. Westport, Conn.: Greenwood, 1979. 42 volumes.

Selected Monographs

Addington, Thomas and Jim Baker. *A Thrilling Episode of Ante-Bellum Days. A True Story of the Oppressed Among Friends and Foes*. Winchester, Ind.: A.C. Beeson & Sons, 1898.

Anderson, John. *The Story of the Life of John Anderson, the Fugitive Slave*. Edited by Harper Twelvetrees. London: Wm. Tweedie, 1863.

Anecdotes and Memoirs of William Boen, A Coloured Man, Who Lived and Died near Mount Holly, New Jersey, to Which Is Added, The Testimony of Friends of Mount Holly Monthly Meeting Concerning Him. Philadelphia: John Richards, 1834.

Aunt Sally; or, The Cross, the way of Freedom. A Narrative of the Slave-life and Purchase of the Mother of Rev. Isaac Williams, of Detroit, Michigan. Cincinnati: American Reform Tract and Book society, 1858.

Bibb, Henry. *Narrative of the Life and Adventures of Henry Bibb, an American Slave*. New York: Author, 1849. A Kentucky narrative.

Brown, John. *Slave Life in Georgia: A Narrative of the Life, Sufferings and Escape of John Brown, A Fugitive Slave....* London: 1855.

Clarke, Lewis Garrard. *Narrative of the Sufferings of Lewis Clarke, During Captivity of More than Twenty-five Years, Among the Algerines of Kentucky....* Boston: David H. Ela, 1845.

[Griffiths, Mattie.] *Autobiography of a Female Slave*. New York: Redfield, 1857.

Hughes, Louis. *Thirty Years a Slave. From Bondage to Freedom. The Institution of Slavery as Seen on the Plantation and in the Home of the Planter*. Milwaukee: South Side Printing, 1897.

Mars, James. *Life of James Mars, A Slave Born and Sold in Connecticut.* Hartford: Case, Lockwood & Co., 1865.

Northup, Solomon. *Twelve Years a Slave. A Narrative of Solomon Northup, a Citizen of New York, Kidnapped in Washington City in 1841 and Rescued in 1853, from a Cotton Plantation near the Red River in Louisiana.* Buffalo: Derby, Orton and Mulligan, 1853.

Smith, Harry ["of Osceola County, Michigan"]. *Fifty Years of Slavery in the United States of America.* Grand Rapids, Mich.: W. Michigan Printing Co., 1891. A Kentucky narrative.

Smith, James L. *Autobiography of James L. Smith....* Norwich, Conn.: Bulletin Co., 1881.

Steward, Austin. *Twenty-two Years a Slave, and Forty Years a Freeman....* Rochester, N.Y.: Wm. Allins, 1857. A Virginia and New York narrative.

Thompson, John. *The Life of John Thompson, A Fugitive Slave.* Worcester, Mass.: Author, 1866.

Watson, Henry. *Narrative of Henry Watson, a Fugitive Slave.* Boston: Bela Marsh, 1848.

Webb, William. *The History of William Wedd.* Detroit: Egbert Hoekstra, 1873. Kentucky narrative.

Webster, Delia A. *Kentucky Jurisprudence. A History of the Trial of Miss Delia A. Webster at Lexington, Kentucky Dec'r 17-21, 1844...on a Charge of Aiding Slav ·· to Escape....* Vergennes: E.W. Blaisdell, 1845.

Williams, James. *Narrative of James Williams, an American Slave, Who was for Several Years a Driver on a Cotton Plantation in Alabama.* New York: American Anti-Slavery Society, 1838.

Miscellaneous

Abajian, James de T. *Blacks in Selected Newspapers, Censuses, and Other Sources: An index to Names and Subjects.* Detroit: Gale, 1977. 3 volumes. Also First Supplement. Detroit: Gale, 1985. 2 volumes.

DeMarce, Virginia Easley. "'Very Slitly Mixt': Tri-Racial Isolate Families of the Upper South—A Genealogical Study." *National Genealogical Society Quarterly* 80:1 (March 1992).

Gutman, Herbert G. *The Black Family in Slavery and Freedom, 1750-1925.* New York Pantheon, 1976. Important contextual information on slave family structure. It contains lengthy transcriptions and family reconstructions from the following plantation slave communities: the Dulles Good Hope Plantation, Orangeburg, South Carolina; Stirling Plantation, Nansemond County, Virginia (see also Kenneth Stampp's Records of Ante-Bellum Southern Plantations, series E, Part 1); the Bennehan-Cameron Plantation, Orange County, North Carolina, (see also Jean B. Anderson's Piedmont Plantation: the Bennehan-Cameron Family and Lands in North Carolina listed in the North Carolina section of this bibliography); and the Henry Watson Plantation, Greene County, Alabama.

Haley, Alex. *Roots.* Garden City, N.Y.: Doubleday, 1976. See also Elizabeth Mills' entry below.

Hamilton, Kenneth Marvin. *Black Towns and Profit. Promotion and Development in the Trans-Appalachian West, 1877-1915.* Chicago: University of Illinois, 1991. Covers Nicodemus, Kansas; Mound Bayou, Mississippi; Langston City, Oklahoma; Boley, Oklahoma; Allensworth, California.

Miller, Randall M. and John David Smith. *Dictionary of Afro-American Slavery.* New York: Greenwood Press, 1988.

Mills, Elizabeth Shown and Gary B. "The Genealogical Assessment of Alex Haley's Roots." *National Genealogical Society Quarterly* 72:1 (March 1984).

Mills, Gary B. "Tracing Free People of Color in the Antebellum South: Methods, Sources and Perspectives." *National Genealogical Society Quarterly* 78:4 (December 1990).

Newman, Debra L. *List of Free Black Heads of Families in the First Census of the United States 1790*. Washington: National Archives, 1973.

Preliminary Inventory of the Records of the Field Offices of the Bureau of Refugees, Freedmen, and Abandoned Lands. Washington, D.C.: National Archives and Records Service, 1973. 3 volumes. See also under state headings for specific Freedmen's Bureau records.

Putney, Martha S. *Runaway Slave Advertisements: A Documentary History from the 1730s to 1790*. Westport, Connecticut: Greenwood, 1983. Four volume set of advertisements from Virginia, North Carolina, Maryland, South Carolina, and Georgia.

Woodson, Carter G. *Free Negro Heads of Families in the United States in 1830*. Washington, D.C.: The Association for the Study of Negro Life and History, 1925.

MILITARY SOURCES

Civil War

Most of the entries in the military section of this bibliography pertain to United States Colored Troops (USCT) units in the Civil War. Over 170,000 African Americans were in these organizations (infantry, cavalry, and artillery), together with African American sailors serving in the U.S. Navy.

1. General

1890 Census for Civil War Veterans and Widows. Microfilm.

Compiled Records Showing Service of Military Units in Volunteer Union Organizations. (Rolls 204-217 of National Archives microfilm record group M594.) These particular rolls contain the compiled records for USCT and other African American Civil War units.

Index to the Compiled Service Records for the United States Colored Troops. Use in conjunction with Dyer below.

Dyer, Frederick H. *A Compendium of the War of the Rebellion*. (Reprint) Dayton, Ohio: Morningside, 1978. Consult this work to determine where specific USCT units were organized and where they served.

Ross, Joseph B. *Tabular Analysis of the Records of the U.S. Colored Troops and Their Predecessor Units in the National Archives of the United States*. Washington, D.C.: National Archives and Records Service, 1973. Useful in tracing unit designations.

2. Published Roster and Indexes

Bates, Samuel P. *History of Pennsylvania Volunteers*. (Reprint) Ann Arbor, Michigan: University Microfilms International, 1982. Volume 5, part 2 contains rosters for the following USCT infantry regiments: 3rd, 6th, 8th, 22nd, 24th, 25th, 32nd, 41st, 43rd, 45th, 127th. The recruits for these regiments were primarily from Pennsylvania.

Callum, Agnes Kane. *Colored Volunteers of Maryland, Civil War, 7th Regiment, United States Colored Troops, 1863-1866*. Baltimore: Mullac, 1990. Transcribed bounty rolls provide names of owners of enlistees.

Connecticut. Adjutant General. *Catalogue of Connecticut Volunteer Organizations*. Hartford, Connecticut, Adjutant General, 1869. Contains rosters for two African American regiments: the 29th Connecticut and the 30th Connecticut (later the 31st USCI). Mostly Connecticut recruits.

Illinois. Adjutant General. Report. Springfield, Illinois: 1886. "Colored Troops" section in volume 8 contains roster for the 29th USCI.

Indiana. Adjutant General. Report. Indianapolis: Adjutant General, 1865-1869. Volume 7 contains roster for the 28th USCI, which was primarily made up of Indiana recruits, although some companies had strong Mid-Atlantic representations. Also listed are Indiana residents in the following USCI regiments: 8th, 13th, 14th, 17th, 23rd, as well as the 4th United States Colored Heavy Artillery.

Iowa. *Roster and Record of Iowa Soldiers in the War of the Rebellion together with Historical Sketches of Volunteer Organizations 1861-1866.* Des Moines, Iowa: Emory English [state printer], 1911. See final volume for roster of 1st Regiment of Iowa African Infantry, later the 60th USCI.

Kansas. Adjutant General. Report. (Reprint) Topeka, Kansas: Hudson, 1896. Rosters for the 1st and 2nd Kansas Colored Volunteer Infantry (later the 79th and 83rd USCI respectively); the 1st, 2nd, and 3rd Kansas Colored Light Artillery and the Independent Colored Kansas Battery (also Light Artillery).

Kentucky. Adjutant General. Report of the Adjutant General of the State of Kentucky. Frankfort, Kentucky: Kentucky Yeoman [printer], 1867. Volume 2 contains rosters for the 5th and 6th United States Colored Cavalry; the 100th, 107th, 108th, 109th, 114th, 115th, 116th, 117th, 118th, 119th, 122nd, 123rd, 124th, 125th, United States Colored Infantry regiments; and the 8th, 12th, and 13th United States Colored Heavy Artillery.

Massachusetts. Adjutant General. *Massachusetts Soldiers, Sailors and Marines in the Civil War.* Brookline, Mass.: Adjutant General, 1931-1935. See the following volumes:
• Volume IV. Contains rosters of the 54th and 55th Massachusetts Volunteer Infantry – recruits from various states.
• Volume VI. Contains 5th Massachusetts Volunteer Cavalry Roster – primarily Massachusetts residents.
• Volume VII. Includes "Massachusetts Soldiers in the United States Colored Troops." Often as not these soldiers were not from Massachusetts, but were recruited by this state's agents to fill its enlist-

ment quotas. The soldiers listed here were primarily recruited at New Bern, North Carolina; Washington, D.C.; Fort Monroe, Virginia; Hilton Head, South Carolina; Nashville, Tennessee; and Vicksburg, Mississippi.

Michigan. Adjutant General. *Record of Service of Michigan Volunteers in the Civil War.* See Volume 46 for roster of the First Michigan Colored Infantry (later the 102nd USCI). See also: *Negroes in Michigan during the Civil War,* published by the Michigan Civil War Centennial Observance Commission.

New Hampshire. Adjutant General. *Revised Register of New Hampshire Soldiers and Sailors in the War of the Rebellion.* Concord, N.H.: Adjutant General, 1895. Includes listings of the USCT recruits credited to New Hampshire in a variety of regiments.

Ohio Roster Commission. *Official Roster of the Soldiers of the State of Ohio in the War of the Rebellion. Various locations and printers, 1886-1893.* See Volume 1, part 2 for rosters of the 5th USCI (the 127th Ohio Volunteer Infantry) and the 27th USCI. Also alphabetical listings of unassigned recruits for the USCT, as well as Ohio recruits for the following USCI regiments: 16th, 17th, 72nd, in addition to the 5th United States Colored Heavy Artillery.

Rhode Island. Adjutant General. Report. Providence, Rhode Island: [Adjutant General], 1866. Contains the roster for the 14th Rhode Island Heavy Artillery (later the 8th and then the 11th U.S. Colored Heavy Artillery). Enlistments from several New England states.

Stryker, William S. *Record of the Officers and Men of New Jersey in the Civil War.* See Volume 2, Part 2 for listings of New Jersey men in various USCI regiments, primarily those raised in New Jersey.

Tennesseans in the Civil War. Nashville, Tennessee: Civil War Commission, 1965. Volume I contains brief regimental histories for the following USCI regiments: 11th (new), 12th, 13th, 14th, 15th, 16th, 17th, 40th,

42nd, 44th, 59th, 61st, 88th (new), 101st; also the following artillery units: batteries A & I of the 2nd United States Colored Light Artillery, and the 1st, 2nd, and 3rd United States Colored Heavy Artillery. Volume II contains a master index.

Wilmer, L. Allison et al. *History and Roster of Maryland Volunteers, War of 1861-5*. (Reprint) Silver Spring, Maryland: Family Line Publications in conjunction with Toomey Press, 1987. Volume 2 contains rosters for the 4th, 7th, 9th, 19th, 30th, and 39th USCI regiments. Also index volume.

3. Regimental Histories and Personal Narratives

Califf, Joseph M. *Record of the Services of the Seventh Regiment U.S. Colored Troops*. Providence, R.I.: Freeman, 1878.

Chenery, William H. *The Fourteenth Regiment Rhode Island Heavy Artillery (Colored) in the War to Preserve the Union 1861-1865*. Rhode Island: Snow & Farnham, 1898.

Cowden, Robert. *A Brief Sketch of the Organization and Services of the Fifty-Ninth Regiment of the United States Colored Infantry and Biographical Sketches*. Dayton: United Brethren, 1883.

Emilio, Luis F. *History of the Fifty-Fourth Regiment of Massachusetts Volunteer Infantry 1863-1865*. Boston: Boston Book, 1891.

Gooding, James Henry. *On the Altar of Freedom: A Black Soldier's Civil War Letters*. Amherst: University of Massachusetts Press, 1991.

Higginson, Thomas Wentworth. *Army Life in a Black Regiment*. (Reprint) Michigan State University, 1960. Covers the 1st South Carolina, later the 33rd USCI.

Newton, Alexander H. *Out of the Briars: An Autobiography and Sketch of the Twenty-Ninth Regiment Connecticut Volunteers*. Philadelphia: A.M.E. Cook Concern, 1910.

Stein, A.H. *History of the Thirty Seventh Regiment United States Colored Infantry.* Philadelphia: King & Baird, 1866.

Tyler, C.M. *Memorials of Lieutenant George H. Wolcott, Late of the Thirtieth United States Colored Troops.* Boston: Sabbath School Society, 1865.

Wilcox, Burt Green. *The 55th Regiment of the Massachusetts Volunteer Infantry.* Brookline, Mass.: 1919.

Revolutionary War

Greene, Robert Ewell. *Black Courage 1775-1783: Documentation of Black Participation in the American Revolution.* Washington: National Society of the Daughters of the American Revolution, 1984.

National Society, Daughters of the American Revolution. "Minority Military Service" series. Also useful for the inclusion of American Indians.
• *Minority Military Service, Connecticut, 1775-1783.* Washington, D.C.: D.A.R., 1988.
• *Minority Military Service, Maine, 1775-1783.* Washington, D.C.: D.A.R., 1990.
• *Minority Military Service, Massachusetts, 1775-1783.* Washington, D.C.: D.A.R., 1989.
• *Minority Military Service, New Hampshire, Vermont, 1775-1783.* Washington, D.C.: 1991.
• *Minority Military Service, Rhode Island, 1775-1783.* Washington: D.A.R., 1988.

Newman, Debra L. *List of Black Servicemen Compiled from the War Department Collection of Revolutionary War Records.* Washington, D.C.: National Archives, 1974.

White, David O. *Connecticut's Black Soldiers 1775-1783.* Chester, Conn.: Pequot, 1973. (Connecticut Bicentennial Series IV.)

Spanish American War

Coston, William Hilary. *The Spanish American War Volunteers 9th U.S. Volunteer Infantry.* Middletown, Pa.: Coston, 1899. Includes roster. Most soldiers enlisted from Louisiana and Texas.

Regular Army

Nankivell, John H. *History of the Twenty-Fifth Regiment United States Infantry 1869-1926.* Fort Collins, Old Army Press, 1972.

LISTINGS ARRANGED BY LOCATION

In compiling the following listings I have tried to limit the citations to titles with clear and immediate genealogical utility, the only exceptions being materials providing a useful historical context for the histories of specific black communities, especially if such titles were rich in biographical information or contained references to named individuals. There are, of course, numerous publications, of genealogical source material and local history containing information on African Americans; however, we have largely confined ourselves to titles concerned solely or in significantly large part with African Americans, although there have been some exceptions when the scope or the quality of the work called for special recognition.

Alabama

Alabama State Census for 1866. This source can be especially important for African American researchers, given its closeness to emancipation. The schedules are segregated and localities within a county are often unspecified. Only heads of household are listed by name. Several counties not included.

Barefield, Marilyn Davis. *Alabama Mortality Schedules 1860.* Easley, S.C.: Southern Historical Press, c1987. The introduction contains a brief but helpful discussion of the enumeration of slave deaths.

Bureau of Refugees, Freedmen and Abandoned Lands. Records of the Assistant Commissioner for Alabama.

Freedmen's Savings and Trust Deposit Ledger Indexes. Microfilm.

Freedmen's Savings and Trust Signature Books. Microfilm.

Hahn, Marilyn Davis (compiler). Alabama Mortality Schedules 1850. Easley, S.C.: Southern Historical. Press, C1983.

Pinkard, Ophelia T. "Blacks Named Wallace in the Federal Census for 1880 and 1900, Shelby County, Alabama." *JAAHGS* 6:4 (winter 1985).

"The Life and Times of Shandy Wesley Jones and Other Freedmen of Tuscaloosa, Alabama." *JAAHGS* 12:3/4 (fall/winter, 1991).

Rathbun, Fred Charles. *Names from Huntsville, Alabama 1865-1869 as Recorded in Registers of Signatures of Depositors in the Huntsville Branch Freedmen's Savings and Trust Company, Accounts 1-385.* Littleton, Colo.: Rathbun, 1986.

Names from Huntsville, Alabama II, 1870 as Recorded in Registers of Signatures of Depositors in the Huntsville Branch, Freedmen's Savings and Trust Company, Accounts 386-791. Littleton, Colorado: Rathbun, 1988.

Arkansas

Bureau of Refugees, Freedmen and Abandoned Lands. Records of the assistant Commissioner for Arkansas. Microfilm.

Records of the Assistant Commissioner for Tennessee. Microfilm.

Freedmen's Savings and Trust Deposit Ledger Indexes. Microfilm.

Freedman's Savings and Trust Signature Books. Microfilm.

Patterson, Ruth Polk. *The Seed of Sally Good'n: A Black Family of Arkansas 1833-1953*. Lexington, Ky.: University Press of Kentucky, 1985. A history of the Polks of Montgomery, Howard, and Pike Counties.

Witherspoon, Dorothy Wofford. *The Homecoming: A Celebration of the Wofford, Lottie, and Brinker Families*. Baltimore: Gateway Press 1990.

California

Beasley, Delilah L. *The Negro Trail Blazers of California: A compilation of Records from the California Archives in the Bancroft Library at the University of California, in Berkeley; and from the diaries, Old Papers and Conversations of Old Pioneers in the State of California*. Los Angeles: 1919.

Inghram, Dorothy. *Beyond All This*. Author, 1983. A family history of the Inghrams in the area of San Bernadino.

Withington, Carol. *The Black Pioneers of Yuba County: The Golden Years*. [Yuba City, Calif.]: Author, 1987.

Connecticut

Brewster-Walker, Sandi J. and Mary McDuffie-Hare (compilers). "Bridgeport, Connecticut Births of Blacks. Abstracts of Records 1855-1864 and 1871-1885." JAAHGS 4:1 (spring 1983).

Brown, Barbra W. and James M. Rose. *Black Roots in Southeastern Connecticut 1650-1900*. Detroit: Gale, 1980.

Delaware

Richards, Mary Fallon. "Black Birth Records, New Castle County, Delaware, 1810-1853." *National Genealogical Society Quarterly* 67:4 (December 1979).

District of Columbia

Brown, Letitia Woods. *Free Negroes in the District of Columbia 1790-1846.*
New York: Oxford University Press, 1972. A scholarly monograph with
the following appendixes: free Negro families in Charles County,
Maryland 1790; occupations of free Negroes before 1835; Negro tax-
payers 1824-1845.

Bureau of Refugees, Freedmen, and Abandoned Lands. Records of the
Assistant Commissioner for District of Columbia. Of special interest:
Reel 16 contains registers of destitute persons. Reel 17 contains case
reports on the destitute. Reels 17 and 18 contain registers of transportation, as well as fairly detailed descriptive lists.

Freedmen's Savings and Trust Deposit Ledger Indexes. Microfilm.

Freedmen's Savings and Trust Signature Books. Microfilm.

Records of the Board of Commissioners for the Emancipation of Slaves in
the District of Colombia 1862-1863. Microfilm. Petitions of owners
and descriptions of slaves are arranged in the Commission minutes.

Records of the United States District Court for the District of Columbia
Relating to Slaves 1851-1863. Microfilm. Contains emancipation
papers resulting from the Act of April 16, 1862. Data from these papers
have been transcribed in the *Journal of Afro-American Historical Society*
(*JAAHGS*), beginning with Vol.1:2. It also contains emancipation
papers resulting from the Act of July 12, 1862, manumission papers
1857-1863, and fugitive slave case papers 1851-1863. Data from the latter are abstracted in *JAAHGS* 2:2.

"Slave Manifest 1833." *Genealogical Magazine of New Jersey* 60:3
(September 1985). Manifest for a cargo of slaves "from port of
Alexandria in the District of Columbia for the port of Natchez in the
State of Misippi Via New Orleans and Norfolk, Virginia." Lists 68
slaves, almost all of whom have surnames, together with listings of ages

and physical descriptions. (Note: Alexandria was formerly part of the District of Columbia, but was ceded to Virginia in 1844.)

Sluby, Paul E. (Sr.). *Genealogy of the Cook Family of Washington, D.C.* Washington: Columbian Harmony Society, 1984.

Holmead's Cemetery (Western Burial Ground), Washington, D.C. Washington: Columbian Harmony Society, 1985.

Mt. Zion Cemetery, Washington, D.C.: Brief History and Interments. Washington: Columbian Harmony Society, 1984.

Woodlawn Cemetery, Washington, D.C.: A Brief History and Inscriptions. Washington: Columbian Harmony Society, 1984.

Sluby, Paul E. (Sr.) and Stanton Workley. *Blacks in the Marriage Records of the District of Columbia Dec. 23, 1811 – Jun. 16, 1870.* Washington: Columbian Harmony Society, 1988.

Walker, Barbara P. "'Colored Residents' Listed in a Washington, D.C. Directory, 1827." *JAAHGS* 9:4 (winter 1988).

Florida

Freedmen's Savings and Trust Deposit Ledger Indexes. Microfilm.

Freedmen's Savings and Trust Signature Books. Microfilm.

Jupiter, Del E. "Augustina and the Kelkers: A Spanish West Florida Line." *National Genealogical Society Quarterly* 80:4 (December 1992).

Phillips, Ulrich Bonnell and James David Glunt (editors). *Florida Plantation Records from the Papers of George Noble Jones.* St. Louis: Missouri, Historical Society, 1927. Jones family plantation records from El Destino and Chemonia plantations in Jefferson County extend form the 1830s to Reconstruction and contain extensive slave and some freedmen records.

Georgia

African-American Family History Association. *Slave Bills of Sale Project.* Atlanta, Ga.: African-American Family History Association, 1986. Two volumes of abstracted and indexed Georgia bills of sale.

Alexander, Adele Logan. *Ambiguous Lives: Free Women of Color in Rural Georgia, 1789-1879.* Fayetteville, Arkansas: University of Arkansas, 1991. Focuses on the Hunts of "Middle Georgia."

Barksdale-Hall, R.C. "The Stevensons: An African-American Family in Slavery and Freedom." *JAAHGS* 6:4 (winter 1985). A Coweta County family.

Bullard, Mary R. *An Abandoned Black Settlement on Cumberland Island, Georgia.* South Dartmouth, Mass.: Author, 1982. Includes transcriptions and analysis of census schedules, also a few genealogies and cemetery transcriptions.

Bureau of Refugees, Freemen and Abandoned Lands. Records of the Assistant Commissioner of Georgia. Microfilm. Contains land titles issued to freedmen, primarily in the Sea Islands.

Clifton, James M. ed. Life and Labor on Argyle Island: Letters and Documents of a Savannah River Rice Plantation 1833-1867. Savannah, Ga.: Beehive, 1978. Letters and other documents of the Manigault family include slave lists at Gowrie and Hermitage plantations.

Coweta County, Georgia Marriages 1827-1979. Newnan-Coweta Historical Society, 1980-1981. Notable for the inclusion of the African American registers, which is unfortunately relatively unusual for such publications. These are found in volume 2.

Freedmen's Savings and Trust Deposit Ledger Index. Microfilm.

Freedmen's Savings and Trust Signature Books. Microfilm.

House, Albert Virgil ed. "Planter Management and Capitalism in Ante-Bellum Georgia." *The Journal of Hugh Fraser Grant, Ricegrower*. New York: Columbia University, 1954. Plantation records from this Glynn County planter cover the years 1834-1861 and include slave lists and vital records.

Nordmann, Chris. "Georgia Registrations of Free People of Color, 1819." *National Genealogical Society Quarterly*, 77:4 (December 1989).

Rathbun, Fred Charles. *Names from Georgia, 1865-1866, Freedmen's Bureau Letters, Roll 13*. Littleton, Colorado: Rathbun, 1986.

Thurmond, Michael L. *A Story Untold: Black Men and Women in Athens History*. *Athens, Ga.*: Clarke County School District, 1978.

"Registry of Free People of Colour, Columbia County Georgia." *JAAHGS* 2:1 [1981].

Wagner, Clarence M. *Profiles of Black Georgia Baptists*. Atlanta: Bennett, 1980. Contains biographical information for local and state Baptist leaders.

Williams, Margo Lee. "Slave Inventory of Elisha Farnell [Pulaski County, Georgia]." *JAAHGS* 12:3/ 4 (fall/winter, 1991).

Illinois

Anderson, H. Obert (Mr. & Mrs.). "Register of Slaves (Indentures) and Emancipation of Slaves." *Illinois State Genealogical of Society Quarterly* 10:1 (spring 1978). Gallatin County records beginning 1814. Series continues in the three subsequent issues of this volume.

Chavers-Wright, Madrue. *The Guarantee*. *P.W. Chavers: Banker, Entrepreneur, Philanthropist in Chicago's Black Belt of the Twenties*. New York: Wright-Armistead, 1985. Useful historical context for Chicago's early twentieth century black belt, as well as information on the Chavers family. Related families: Baker, Bannister, Calloway and Pannell.

Chicago Edition *Black's Blue Book* (1923-1924).

Colored People's Blue Book and Business Directory of Chicago, Illinois 1905. Chicago, Ill.: Celebrity, 1905.

Eisenberg, Marcia. "Blacks in the 1850 Federal Census, City of Chicago, Cook County, Illinois." *JAAHGS* beginning 6:1 (spring 1985).

Furgal, Suzanne Kersten. "Blacks in the First and Second Wards of Chicago, Illinois as Found in the 1860 Federal Census." *JAAHGS* 6:3 (fall 1985).

"Black and Mulattoes in the 1860 Federal Census: City of Chicago, Third and Fourth Wards." *JAAHGS* 8:2 (summer 1987).

"Blacks and Mulattoes in Wards Eight, Nine and Ten of Chicago, Cook County, Illinois." *JAAHGS* 6:3 (fall 1985).

Grossman, James. *Land of Hope*. Chicago, Black Southerners and the Great Migration. Chicago: University of Chicago, 1989. Provides historical context for working with African American migration to Chicago in the early twentieth century.

Husband, Lori. *Chicago World War I Draftees: Districts 3,4,5 and 70*. Oak Forest, Ill.: Husband, 1990.

Deaths in the Chicago Defender 1910-1920. Park Forest, Ill.: Husband, 1990.

Muelder, Hermann R. *A Hero Come Home from War: Among the Black Citizens of Galesburg, Illinois, 1860-1880*. Galesburg, Ill.: Knox College Library, 1987. Focuses on community spokesman Joseph Barquet and other veterans of the 54th Massachusetts Volunteer Infantry.

Pratt, Mildred. *We the People Tell Our Story: Bloomington-Normal Black History Project*. Normal, Ill.: Bloomington-Normal Black History Project, 1987.

Sanders, Walter R. "The Negro in Montgomery County, Illinois." *Illinois State Genealogical Society Quarterly* 10:1 (spring 1978).

Tregillis, Helen Cox. *River Roads to Freedom: Fugitive Slave Notices and Sheriff Notices Found in Illinois Sources.* Bowie, Md.: Heritage, 1988.

Williams, Nola Jones. *Lincoln School Memories: A History of Blacks in Edwardsville, Illinois.* Wheaton, Ill.: Williams, 1986. Madison County local history.

Williams, Rick D. "African American Churches in Bloomington-Normal, Illinois: 100 Years Reflecting the Black Church in America." *JAAHGS* 12:3/4 (fall/winter 1991).

Indiana

Bigham, Darrel E. *We Ask Only a Fair Trial: A History of the Black Community of Evansville, Indiana.* Bloomington, Ind.: Indiana University Press, 1987. Does not contain genealogical source material or family histories; however, many individuals are mentioned in the text and are indexed. Of interest to anyone with roots in Evansville for the historical context it establishes.

"Negro Registers." *Hoosier Genealogist* 17:2 (June 1977). Registers of free blacks in 1853 in Bartholomew, Franklin, and Jennings Counties.

Robbins, Coy D. *African Heritage in Morgan County, Indiana.* Bloomington, Ind.: Indiana African American Historical and Genealogical Society, 1991.

"Freedom Papers Found in Orange County, Indiana." *JAAHGS* 7:3 (fall 1986).

"Negro Register Orange County, Indiana (1853-1861)." *JAAHGS* 7:2 (summer 1986).

"Orange County, Indiana Black Americans in World War I." *JAAHGS* 8:2 (summer 1987).

Spears, Jean E. *Admission Record, Indianapolis Asylum of Friendless Colored Children, 1871-1900.* Indianapolis: Indiana Historical Society, 1978.

Thornbrough, Emma Lou. *The Negro in Indiana. A Study of a Minority.* Indianapolis: Indiana Historical Bureau, 1957.

Witcher, Curt B. "Allen County, Indiana, Black American in World War I." *JAAHGS* 8:3 (fall 1987).

Kansas

Marshall, Marguerite Mitchell. *An Account of Afro-Americans in Southeast Kansas 1884-1984.* Manhattan, Kans.: Wheatland Books, 1984.

United States. Department of the Interior. *Promised Land on the Solomon. Black Settlement at Nicodemus, Kansas.* [Denver, Colorado?]: Dept. of the Interior, 1986.

Kentucky

"And Take Unto Themselves the Surname of 'Isbell.' Floyd County, 1825." *Kentucky Ancestors* 22:2 (autumn 1986). Manumissions of slaves belonging to William James Mayo.

Ballardo, Lewis J. (Jr.) "Frankfort, Kentucky Census of Free Blacks, 1842." *National Genealogical Society Quarterly* 63:4 (December 1975).

Bogardus, Carl R. (Sr.) "Black Marriages, Gallatin County, Kentucky, 1866 to 1913." *JAAHGS* 2,3, and 4 (summer, fall, and winter 1981).

Brown, Richard. "Free Blacks of Boyle County, Kentucky 1850-1860. A Research Note." *The Register of the Kentucky Historical Society* 87:4 (Autumn 1989).

"Communication from the Commissioner of Freedmen's Affairs Transmitting Petition of Colored People of Kentucky in Relation to Unjust Taxation by State Authority." Serial Set 40th Congress 2nd Session (1867-1868), House Documents Vol. 9, No. 70. A petition from freedmen of Daviess County.

Dearing, David E. "Freedmen's Bureau Records from Landrum's List of Stanford Children anxious for School–Henderson County Indentures." *JAAHGS* 10:4 (winter 1989).

Dunningan, Alice Allison. *The Fascinating Story of Black Kentuckians: Their Heritage and Traditions.* Washington, D.C.: Associated Publishers, 1982. Much biographical information on prominent African Americans from the early history of the state to the present day.

Freedmen's Savings and Trust Deposit Ledger Indexes. Microfilm.

Freedmen's Savings and Trust Signature Books. Microfilm.

Garrison, Gwendolyn. *Black Marriage Bonds of Fayette County, Kentucky 1866-1876.* Lexington, Ky.: Kentucky Tree-Search, 1985.

Hill, Margaret Lester. "Index to Black Marriages Barren County, Kentucky 1866-1875." *JAAHGS* beginning 4:3 (fall 1983).

"Kentucky Marriage Records." *JAAHGS* 1:1 (summer 1980). Records for African Americans in Todd, Daviess, and McCracken Counties.

Lloyd, Emma Rouse. *Clasping Hands with Generations Past.* Cincinnati: Lloyd, 1932. Contains brief section entitled "Our Colored Folk," giving information on the slaves of the Hendersons of Crittenden, Grant County. Surnames mentioned include Robinson, Sechrist, Smith, Williams, and Harrison.

"Monument to Franklin County's Black Civil War Soldiers." *Kentucky Ancestors* 20:1 (summer 1984).

Peters, Frank Norman R. "Free Black Residents of Logan County, Kentucky, 1850." *Kentucky Ancestors* 23:3 (winter 1988).

Robinson, Lottie Offett. *The Bond-Washington Story. The Education of Black People in Elizabethtown, Kentucky.* Georgetown, Ky.: Kreative Grafiks [printer], 1983. Many Individuals included in the history of black education in the county seat of Hardin County.

Sanders, Carol L. *Russell County, Kentucky Marriages Book I 1866-1875.* Blue Ash, Ohio: Sanders, 1988.

Russell County, *Kentucky Black Marriages Book II 1876-1914.*

Schreiner-Yantis, Nettie. See Virginia listings.

Thackery, David T. "Thomas McDougal, A Kentucky Freedman." *Origins* (Newberry Library) 3:1 (November 1986). Reprinted *Genealogical Journal* 15:3.

Tippie, Gwendolyn. *Afro-American Births of Adair Thru Ballard County, Kentucky 1852-1862.* Also, *Afro-American Births of Adair thru Bath County 1852-1862*; *Afro-American Births of Barren thru Bath County 1852-1862*; *Afro-American Births of Boone thru Bourbon County 1852-1862*; *Afro-American Births of Boyle thru Caldwell County 1852-1862*; *Afro-American Births of Boone thru Boyle County 1852-1862.*

Vanderpool, Montgomery. *Colored Marriage Bonds*, Logan County, Kentucky to 1900. Russellville, Ky.: Vanderpool, 1985.

Louisiana

Barnette, Mic. "William Marshall of Baton Rouge and his Descendants." *National Genealogical Society Quarterly* 73:1 (March 1985).

Bureau of Refugees, Freedmen and Abandoned Lands. Records of the Assistant Commissioner for Louisiana. Microfilm. Contains "reports of indigents" organized by parish. Early reports for African Americans give name of former owner and age. Contains register of applications by freedmen for abandoned land.

Records of the Assistant Commissioner for Mississippi. Microfilm. Marriage registers for Vicksburg, Davis Bend, and Natchez contain numerous entries for Louisiana freedmen living in parishes across the Mississippi River from these locations.

Records of the Freedmen's Hospital and New Orleans Area Field Office of the Bureau of Refugees, Freedmen and Abandoned Lands 1865-1869. Microfilm. Field office records for Iberville, Orleans, Plaquemines, St. Bernard, and West Baton Rouge Parishes.

Burton, Willie. *On the Black Side of Shreveport.* Author, 1983. Contains much biographical information.

Davis, Edwin Adams. *Plantation Life in the Florida Parishes of Louisiana 1836-1846 as Reflected in the Diary of Bennet H. Barrow.* New York: Columbia University, 1943.

DeVille, Winston. *Slaves and Masters of Pointe Coupe, Louisiana. A Calendar of Civil Records 1762-1823.* Ville Platte, La.: DeVille, 1988.

Freedmen's Savings and Trust Deposit Ledger Indexes. Microfilm.

Freedmen's Savings and Trust Signature Books. Microfilm.

Hebert, Donald J. *Southwest Louisiana Records: Church and Civil Records.* Baton Rouge, La.: Claitor's, 1973-1984. Multi-volume series. Volume 2, pp. xii-xx; volume 3, pp. 684-694; and volume 33, pp. 106-307 are of special interest.

Knight, Carol Young. *First Settlers of Catahoula Parish, Louisiana 1808-1839.* Aledo, Texas: Knight, 1983. Primarily records for the sale of land and slaves, who are usually referred to by name.

Mills, Elizabeth Shown. "de Mezieres-Trichel-Grappe: A Study of a Tri-caste Lineage in the Old South." *The Genealogist* 6:1 (spring 1985).

"Slaves and Masters: The Louisiana Metoyers." *National Genealogical Society Quarterly* 70:3 (September 1982).

Stephenson, Wendell Holmes and Isaac Franklin. *Slave Trader and Planter of the Old South with Plantation Records.* University, La.: Louisiana State University Press, 1938. Contains extensive slave records from Franklin's plantation in West Feliciana Parish during the years 1846-1850.

Xavier University. *Guide to the Heartman Manuscripts on Slavery.* Boston: G.K. Hall, 1982. A guide and calendar to the Heartman collection on slavery, housed at Xavier University, New Orleans. Bills of sale and other documents pertaining to slaves, as well as materials concerning free blacks (primarily in Louisiana) are described. Thorough indexing.

Maryland

Bragg, George F. *Men of Maryland.* Baltimore: Church Advocate Press, 1925. Biographies of prominent Maryland African Americans of the nineteenth and early twentieth centuries.

Brown, Letitia Woods. See under District of Columbia.

Clayton, Ralph. *Black Baltimore 1820-1870.* Bowie, Md.: Heritage Books, 1987. Includes index of advertisements for runaway slaves in *The Baltimore Sun* 1837-1864, Laurel Cemetery interments 1852-1858, 1870 census index for black families of East Baltimore.

Free Blacks of Ann Arundel County, Maryland 1850. Bowie, Md.: Heritage Books, 1987.

Cornelison, Alice. "History of Blacks in Howard County, Maryland." *JAAHGS* 10:2/3 (summer and fall 1989).

Freedmen's Savings and Trust Deposit Ledger Indexes. Microfilm.

Freedmen's Savings and Trust Signature Books. Microfilm.

Green, Fletcher M. ed. *Ferry Hill Plantation Journal January 4, 1838- January 15, 1839*. Chapel Hill, N.C.: University of North Carolina Press, 1961 (volume 43 of James Sprunt Studies in History and Political Science). Journal of John Blackford of Washington County, Maryland. Contains no slave lists, but journal entries frequently mention slaves by name.

Jacobsen, Phebe R. "Assessment of Slaves, District 1, Talbot County, Maryland, 1832." *JAAHGS* 4:2 (summer 1983).

Lucas, Townsend M. "Fairmount Heights, Prince George's County, Maryland. A 1910 Census Construction with Historical Notes." *JAAHGS* 9:1 (spring 1988).

Meyer, Mary K. *Free Blacks in Hereford, Somerset and Talbot Counties, Maryland 1832*. Mt. Airy, Md.: Pipe Creek Publisher, 1991.

"Manumission of William Cromwell and others, Ann Arundel County, Maryland, 1854." *JAAHGS* 9:4 (winter 1988).

Quander, Rohulamin. "The Quander Family 1684-1910," *JAAHGS* 3:2 (summer 1982).

Provine, Dorothy S. *Registrations of Free Negroes 1806-1863, Prince George's County, Maryland*. Washington, D.C.: Columbian Harmony Society, 1990.

Russell, George Ely. "Black Baptism and Marriage Records, Frederick County, Maryland, 1787-1870." *JAAHGS* 2:1.

Slezak, Eva. "Black Householders in the 1810 Baltimore City Directory." *JAAHGS* 5:2 (summer 1984).

Thomas, Sammie L. *The Books of the Families of the African Diaspora. Volume of the Families Between the Atlantic and the Chesapeake.* Washington, D.C.: Sammie L. Thomas, 1990. Families covered: Barkley, Brewington, Coulbourne. Furniss, Harmon, Haymon, Maddox, Shelton, Spence, Stanford, Tighman, White.

Massachusetts

Carvalho, Joseph (III). *Black Families in Hampden County, Massachusetts 1650-1855.* Boston: New England Historic Genealogical Society and Institute for Massachusetts Studies (Westfield State College), 1984.

Holly, H. Hobart. "Records of Blacks and Indians in Old Braintree, Massachusetts." *The New England Historical and Genealogical Register* 140:2 (April 1986).

Lainhart, Ann S. "Descendants of Cuff Ashport of Bridgewater, Massachusetts." *JAAHGS* 11:3 (fall 1990).

Russell, Donna Valley. "The Abrahams of Natick and Grafton, Massachusetts." *JAAHGS* 5:2 (summer 1984).

Michigan

DeVries, James E. *Race and Kinship in a Midwestern Town. The Black Experience in Monroe, Michigan 1900-1915.* Chicago: University of Illinois, 1984. Academic orientation, but includes several detailed "family reconstruction" in an appendix.

Directory of Negro Businesses, Professions and Churches for Detroit and Environs. Detroit: Associates Advertisers' Service, [1952]. Microfiche.

Stewart, Roma Jones. "The Migration of a Free People. Cass County's Black Settlers from North Carolina." *Michigan History* 71:1 (January/February 1987).

Warren, Francis H. *Michigan Manual of Freedmen's Progress*. Detroit, 1915. Contains biographical information.

Mississippi

Alford, Terry L. "Some Manumissions Recorded in the Adams County Deed Books in Chancery Clerk's Office, Natchez, Mississippi, 1795-1835." *Journal of Mississippi History* 33:1 (February 1981).

Bureau of Refugees, Freedmen and Abandoned Lands. Records of the Assistant Commissioner for Tennessee. Microfilm. Contains labor contracts for Bolivar County, Mississippi.

Records for the Assistant Commissioner for Mississippi. Microfilm. The marriages recorded here were performed during the years 1864 and 1865 in Vicksburg, Natchez, and Davis Bend. An extensive collection of freedmen labor contracts are also found here. Unfortunately the order of their arrangements makes research difficult.

Evans, W.A. "Free Negroes in Monroe County During Slavery." *Journal of Mississippi History* 10:3 (January 1941). Contains a few references to individuals by name.

Freedman's Saving and Trust Deposit Ledger Indexes. Microfilm.

Freedman's Savings and Trust Signature Books. Microfilm.

Genealogical Society of Utah. Microfilm copies of manuscript marriage records for the following counties:
- Alcorn (old Tishomingo) 1866-1921 "colored registers."
- Bolivar 1853-1920 "colored and white registers."
- Clarke 1865-1919 "freedmen registers."
- George 1910-1921 "colored registers."
- Franklin 1871-1928 "colored registers."
- Lauderdale 1870-1916 "marriage record, colored."

Griffith, Lucille ed. "Notes and Documents: The Plantation Record Book of Brookdale Farm, Amite County, 1856-1857." *Journal of Mississippi History* 7:1 (January 1945). Journal of the Reverend Hamiton McKnight contains no slave lists but contains frequent references to slaves by name.

Hamilton, William B. and William D. McCain. "Wealth in the Natchez Region: Inventories of the Estate of Charles Percy, 1794 and 1804." *Journal of Mississippi History* 10:3 (July 1948). Includes slave lists.

Mississippi Index (Soundex) to Marriages Prior to 1926 (Mixed Colors). Microfilm.

"Oldham Slave Case: Correspondence and Documents." Manuscripts dates 1857-1860 concerning the emancipation of two slaves named Syrene and Emeline by their owner, James Oldham of Coahoma County.

Phillips, Mark A. *Alexander Davis and Della Watkins: The Story of One Black Couple from Mississippi with Note on Some of their Descendants.* [Houston, Texas?]: Phillips, 1988.

Riley, Franklin L. ed. "Diary of a Mississippi Planter, January 1, 1840 to April, 1863." Publications of the Mississippi Historical Society, volume 10 (1909). Diary of Dr. Martin W. Philips of Hinds County includes references to his slaves. Births and deaths frequently noted.

Sewell, George A. and Margaret L. Dwight. *Mississippi Black History Makers.* Jackson, Miss.: University Press of Mississippi, 1984. Extensive biographical compendium of prominent African Americans.

Thompson, Julius E. *The Black Press in Mississippi 1865-1985. A Directory.* West Cornwall, Conn.: Locust Hill Press, 1988. Bibliographic listings arranged by county of publication. Holding information is provided, although in many cases apparently no extant copies have survived. In other instances the only extant copies are in private hands.

ADDENDUM. The state of Mississippi mandated the enumeration of educable children. These special school censuses can have great genealogical value.

Enumeration of Educable Children, Lauderdale County, Mississippi School Census, 1885, White and Black. Meridian, Miss.: Lauderdale County Dept. of Archives and History, 1987.

Fox, Louise C. *Educable Children, Tate County, Mississippi 1894.* Senatobia, Mississippi, Tate County, Mississippi Genealogical and Historical Society, [1987?].

Jackson County, Mississippi School Census 1912. Ocean Springs Genealogical Society, 1989.

Smith, Rebecca Haas. *Educable Children, Tate County, Mississippi, 1892.* Senatobia, Miss.: Tate County Mississippi Genealogical and Historical Society, 1897.

Missouri

Bartels, Carolyn M. *Cooper County Colored Marriages 1865-1866.* Shawnee Mission, Kans.: Bartels, [198_?].

Freedmen's Savings and Trust Deposit Ledger Indexes. Microfilm.

Freedmen's Savings and Trust Signature Books. Microfilm.

O'Dell, Charles. *Black Households in Columbia, Missouri 1901-1909: A Directory Along with a List of All Black Residents of Boone County in 1905.* Columbia, Mo.: O'Dell, 1988.

Peters, Norman R. "The Farris Family of Pike County, Missouri." *JAAGHS* 8:4 (winter 1987).

New Jersey

Brown, Virginia Alleman. "Warren and Sussex Counties Slave Births 1804-1833." *The Genealogical Magazine of New Jersey* 54:2/3 (May/September 1979).

Hoff, Henry B. See listing under New York.

New York

Caro, Edythe Quinn. *"The Hills" in Mid-Nineteenth Century. The History of a Rural Afro-American Community in Westchester County, New York.* Valhalla, New York: Westchester County Historical Society, 1988.

Eichholz, Alice and James M. Rose. *Free Black Heads of Households in the New York State Federal Census 1790-1830.* Detroit: Gale, 1981.

"New York State Manumissions." *New York Genealogical and Biographical Record* 108:4 (October 1977) – 110:1 (January 1979).

Eisenberg, Marcia Jesiek. "Seneca County, New York Afro-Americans in the Federal Census." *JAAHGS* beginning 7:2 (summer 1986). Begins with abstracts from 1810 and 1820 schedules. Subsequent issues continue with census years up through 1850.

Freedmen's Savings and Trust Deposit Ledger Indexes. Microfilm.

Freedmen's Savings and Trust Signature Books. Microfilm.

Gallagher, Kevin J. "Inmates of the City Almshouse, Poughkeepsie, New York." *JAAHGS* 2:1 (spring 1981). African American inmates mid to late 19th century.

"Registers of Births of Slaves." *JAAHGS* 2:2 (summer 1981). Records from Poughkeepsie, New York.

Heidgerd, William. *Black History of New Paltz*. New Paltz, N.Y.: Elting Memorial Library, 1986.

Hoff, Henry B. "A Colonial Black Family in New York and New Jersey: Peiter Santomee and His Descendants." *JAAHGS* 9:3 (fall 1988). "Additions and Corrections" in 10:4 (winter 1989).

Marcus, Grania Bolton. *A Forgotten People: Discovering the Black Experience in Suffolk County*. Setuaket, N.Y.: Society for the Preservation of Long Island Antiquities, 1988.

"The Negro in Dutchess County in the Eighteenth Century." *Dutchess County Historical Society Year Book* (1941).

North Carolina

Anderson, Jean Bradley. *Piedmont Plantation: The Bennehan-Cameron Family and Lands in North Carolina*. Durham, N.C.: Historic Preservation Society of Durham, 1985.

Blackman, A.M. *Cohabitation Records of Davie County, North Carolina, 1866*. Clemmons, N.C.: Blackman, 1987.

Braswell, Peggy Jo. "Halifax County Free Persons of Color." *North Carolina Afro-American Historical and Genealogical Society Quarterly* 5:2 (summer 1990).

Bridges, Kathryn L. "Black Members of St. John's Evangelical Lutheran Church, Cabarrus County, North Carolina 1858-1859." *North Carolina Genealogical Society Journal* 6:3 (August 1980).

Bureau of Refugees, Freedmen and Abandoned Lands. *Records of the Assistant Commissioner for North Carolina*. Microfilm. Reports ration distribution receipts and indication number of adults and children under name of head of household. Lists of large groups of freedmen being transported to Louisiana, Texas, Arkansas, Mississippi, and Tennessee. Labor contracts.

Cunningham, Glenn. "The Hidden Lives of Waverly Plantation." *JAAHGS* 11:1/2 (spring and fall 1990). Person County plantation records.

Davenport, David Paul. "The Record of a Sampson County Slave Family 1781-1836." *North Carolina Genealogical Society Journal* 15:1 (February 1989). Slaves belonging to the Toole family.

Franklin, John Hope. *The Free Negro in North Carolina 1790-1860.* New York: Russell & Russell, 1943. A scholarly work with a useful bibliography. A "must read" for anyone with free black North Carolina ancestry. Brief appendixes include lists of free blacks having property valued at more than $2,500 in 1860; also free black owners of slaves in 1790, 1830, and 1860.

Freedmen's Savings and Trust Deposit Ledger Indexes. Microfilm. Contains indexes for New Bern, Raleigh, and Wilmington.

Freedmen's Savings and Trust Signature Books. Microfilm 709. Reel 18 contains records for New Bern, Raleigh, and Wilmington. (Also see Tetterton below.)

Hairston, Peter W. *The Cooleemee Plantation and its People.* Lexington, N.C.: Davidson County Community College, 1986. A history of the Hairston plantation in Davie and Davidson Counties. Extensive slave records.

Heinegg, Paul. *Free African Americans of North Carolina, Including the History of More than 80% of those Counted as "All Other Free Persons" in the 1790 and 1800 Census.* Abqaiq, Saudi Arabia: Heinegg, 1992. (Third revised edition.)

Slave Marriages in Northampton County, North Carolina and the Location of their Families in the 1870 and 1880 Census. Abqaiq, Saudi Arabia: Heinegg, 1988.

Henry, Phillip M. "Early Black Entrepreneurs and Entrepreneurship in Durham and Winston-Salam." *North Carolina Afro-American Historical and Genealogical Society Quarterly* 6:1 (summer 1991).

Heritage of Blacks in North Carolina. Charlotte, N.C.: North Carolina African-American Heritage Foundation, 1900.

Johnston, Hugh Buckner (Jr.). "Some Bible and Other Family Records, Part 1." *North Carolina Genealogical Society Journal* 7:4 (November 1981). Slave vital records in Bibles of the following families: Applewhite (Wilson County), Barnes (Nash County), Harris (Pitt County), and Pender (Edgecombe County).

Kent, Harriette Thorne. *Swampers: Free Blacks and the Great Dismal Swamp*. Author, 1991. Law mandated the registration of free blacks working in the Great Dismal, together with a physical description. These records come from the counties Camden, Chowan, Gates, Halifax, and Pasquotank.

Linn, Jo White. "Accounts of Slaves in the Estate of John Pool." *Rowan County Register* 5:3 (August 1990).

"Rowan County Marriage Register 1851-1868." *Rowan County Register* 2:2 (May 1897). Includes freedmen cohabitation bonds.

McLain, Geraldine. *The Iredell Marriage Records (1851-1885)*. Statesville, N.C.: Genealogical Society of Iredell County, 1987. Includes freedmen cohabitation bonds (1866) and black marriage records 1867-1882.

"Melchor Slave Record (1821-1864)." *North Carolina Genealogical Society Quarterly* 13:4 (November 1987). Slaves of Christopher Melchor, Cabarrus County.

Mobley, Joe A. *James City: A Black Community in North Carolina 1863-1900*. Raleigh, N.C.: North Carolina Division of Archives and History, 1981. History of a freemen community in the vicinity of New Bern.

North Carolina Afro-American Historical and Genealogical Quarterly.

North Carolina Division of Archives and History. *An Index to Marriage Bonds Filed in North Carolina State Archives.* Microfiche. Covers period 1741-1868. Contains references to a few freedmen and antebellum free black marriages.

The following county records are also on North Carolina Division of Archives and History microfilm:
- Bertie County "Cohabitation Records, 1866."
- Catawba County "Freedmen's Marriage Record 1866."
- Catawba County marriage register "Black 1867-1872."
- Duplin County marriage register "Colored Male and Female 1952-1962; Marriage of Freed People 1866."
- Forsyth County "Acknowledgement of Cohabitation 1820-1866."
- Granville County "Marriages of Freed People 1866"; "Marriage Register 1867-1924."
- Mecklenburg County "Marriage Records (Colored) 1850-1867."
- Pasqutank County "Account Book, Cohabitation of Negroes 1856-1867."
- Pequimans County "Record of Marriages by Freedmen 1866-1867."

Perry, Matthew Leary. "The Negro in Fayetteville" in *The Story of Fayetteville* by John A. Oates (Oates, 1950).

Pritchford, Shirley. "Thomas J. Pritchford Slave List." *North Carolina Genealogical and Historical Society Quarterly* 5:2 (summer 1990). Bible record of Thomas Pritchford of Wake County.

Redford, Dorothy Spruill. *Somerset Homecoming. Recovering a Lost Heritage.* New York: Doubleday, 1988. Slave families in the area of Great Dismal Swamp.

"Registration of Marriage of Persons, Lately Slaves, 1866, Randolph County, North Carolina." *North Carolina Afro-American Historical and Genealogical Society Quarterly* 6:1 (spring 1991).

Smith, Gloria L. *The Route Taken. The Migration of One Group of African-American Settlers from North Carolina to Texas after the Civil War.* Tucson, Ariz.: Trailstones, 1990.

Stewart, Roma Jones. "Research in Progress: Free Blacks in Antebellum America." *Origins* (Newberry Library) 4:1 (December 1987). See also same author under Michigan.

Taylor, Anne Hatcher. *Black Cemetery Records, Reunions and Personality Sketches, Hertford and Gates Counties 1850-1988.* Winston, N.C.: Hatcher-Taylor, 1988.

Tetterton, Beverly, ed. *North Carolina Freedman's Savings and Trust Records.* Abstracted by Bill Reaves. Raleigh, N.C.: North Carolina Genealogical Society, 1992.

Watson, C.H. *Colored Charlotte.* Published in Connection with the Fiftieth Anniversary of the Freedom of the Negro in the County of Mecklenberg and the City of Charlotte, North Carolina. Charlotte, N.C.: A.M.E.Zion Job Print, 195. Microfiche.

White, Barnetta McGhee. *In Search of Kith and Kin: The History of a Southern Black Family.* Baltimore: Gateway, 1986. A genealogy of the McGhees of Granville County.

Wynne, Frances Holloway. "Confederate Tax Assessments for Rowan County, North Carolina, 1863." *JAAHGS* beginning 7:2 (summer 1986).

"Free Black Inhabitants of Wake County, North Carolina." *JAAHGS* 1:2 (LHF open shelf).

Ohio

Buchanan, James. *The Blacks of Pickaway County, Ohio in the Nineteenth Century.* Bowie, Md: Heritage, 1988.

Clay, Sheila Farmer. *A Brief History of St. Paul A.M.E. Church, Urbana, Ohio.* Clay, 1987.

"Certificates of Freedom – Ross County and Champaign County, Ohio." *JAAHGS* 8:4 (winter 1987).

Early Death Record (Blacks Only) Volumes 1 & 2. Champaign County, Ohio 1867-1909. Dayton, Ohio: Clay, (1987?).

Burial Records: G.F. Allen & Company: 15 Jan. 1933 –30 Oct. 1967 Urbana, Ohio. Dayton, Ohio: Clay, 1983. Records of a Champaign County black mortician contain important genealogical information.

Dabney, Wendell Phillips. *Cincinnati's Colored Citizens: Historical, Sociological and Biographical.* Cincinnati: Ohio Book Store, c. 1926 (1988 reprint).

Dennis, James L. *Washington's Darker Brother: One Hundred Years of Black History in Washington County, Ohio 1788-1888.* Dennis, 1986.

Houseman, Michael L. "Belmont County, Ohio, Census of Blacks, 1863." *National Genealogical Society Quarterly* 69:3 (September 1981).

Jones, David T. *Pioneer Blacks in Adams County, Ohio.* Wabash, Ind.: Decamp, 1963.

Lucas, Ernestine Grant. *From Paris to Springfield: The Slave Connection Basye-Basey.* Decorah, Iowa: Anundsen [printer], 1983. Traces the Baseys of Springfield, Ohio back to Missouri and Kentucky.

Nitchman, Paul E. *Blacks in Ohio, 1880.* Decorah, Iowa: Anundsen [printer], 19850. Ongoing series of census transcriptions. volume 1: Adams-Carroll Counties; volume 2: champaign-Clinton Counties; Volume 3: Columbiana-Fayette Counties; volume 4: Franklin-Geauga Counties; volume 5: City of Cincinnati; volume 6: Green-Henry Counties; volume 7: Highland-Lorain Counties.

Ohio Historical Society. *Blacks Immigrating to Ohio 1861-1863.* Columbus, Ohio: Ohio Historical Society, 1988. Microfilm.

Overton, Julie M. "Blacks in the 1850 Federal Census of Greene County, Ohio." *JAAHGS* 3:4 (winter 1982).

Snider, Wayne L. *Guernsey County's Black Pioneers, Patriots and Persons.* Columbus, Ohio: Ohio Historical Society, 1979.

Turpin, Joan. *Register of Black, Mulatto, and Poor Persons in four Ohio Counties 1791-1861.* Bowie, Md.: Heritage Books, 1985. The counties in question are Clinton, Highland, Logan, and Ross. The records were generated by an Ohio law requiring all black or mulatto persons to appear before the clerk of the county common pleas court to prove free status with appropriate documentation.

Weisman, Kay. "1863 Special Enumeration of Blacks in Ohio: Abstract of the Meigs County Census." *JAAHGS* 2:3 (fall 1981).

Woodson, Minnie Shumate. "Black and Mulatto Persons in Jackson County, Ohio." *JAAHGS* 5:1 (spring 1984). Covers years 1818-1854.

Oklahoma (Indian Territory)

Index of Final Rolls of Citizens and Freedmen of the Five Civilized Tribes in the Indian Territory. Listings include African Americans affiliated with the Seminoles, Cherokees, Creeks, Choctaws, and Chickasaws.

Pennsylvania

Dillard, Thomas Henry. "History of Calumet Lodge #25 Free and Accepted Masons, Prince Hall Affiliation, Farrell, Mercer County, Pennsylvania." *JAAHGS* 10:1 (January 1989).

Freedmen's Savings and Trust Deposit Ledger Indexes. Microfilm.

Freedmen's Saving and Trust Signature Books. Microfilm.

Fries, Stella M., et al. *Some Chambersberg Roots: A Black Perspective.* Fries, 1980.

Hawbaker, Gary T. *Runaways, Rascals, and Rogues: Missing Spouses, Servants and Slaves.* Abstracts from Lancaster County Pennsylvania Newspapers. Hershey, Pa.: Haebaker, 1987.

Nash, Gary B. *Forging Freedom: The Formation of Philadelphia's Black Community, 1720-1840.* Cambridge, Mass: Harvard, 1988.

Negro Register 1792-1851 Washington County, Pennsylvania. Photocopied from original in the office of the Recorder of Deeds, Washington, Washington County, Pennsylvania.

Palmer, Ronald D. "A Short History of the Black Population in the Region of Mt. Pleasant, Pennsylvania." *JAAHGS* 12:3/4 (fall and winter,1991).

Ruffin, C. Bernard. "Records of the Sellers Funeral Home, Chambersburg, Pennsylvania Relating to Black Families of Franklin County, 1866-1933." *JAAHGS* beginning 3:2 (summer 1982).

Smith, Billy G. and Richard Wojtowicz. *Blacks Who Stole Themselves: Advertisements for Runaways in the Pennsylvania Gazette 1728-1790.* Philadelphia: University of Pennsylvania, 1989.

Rhode Island

Battle, Charles A. *Negroes on the Island of Rhode Island.* Newport, R.I: Black Museum, (1932?).

Beaman, Alden G. "Rhode Island Black Genealogy Inscriptions from the Negro Section of the Common Burial Ground, Newport." *Rhode Island Genealogical Register* 8:2 (October 1985).

South Carolina

Arnold, Jonnie B. *Index to 1860 Mortality Schedule of South Carolina.* Greenville, S.C.: Arnold, 1982. Includes indexing for slaves, indicating names of owners if that information is present in the schedules.

Bell, Malcom (Jr). *Major Butler's Legacy: Five Generations of a Arnold, Jonnie. Index to 1860 Mortality Schedule of South Carolina.* Greenville, S.C: Arnold, 1982. Includes indexing for slaves, indicating names of owners if that information is also present in the schedules.

Bureau of Refugees, Freedmen and Abandoned Lands. Records of the Assistant Commissioner for South Carolina. Microfilm.

Cody, Cheryll Ann. *Slave Demography and Family Formation: A Community Study of the Bell Family Plantations, 1720-1896.* (Ph.D. dissertation, University of Minnesota, 1982). Microfilm.

"There was no 'Absalom' on the Ball plantations: Slave-naming Practices in the South Carolina Low Country, 1720-1865." *American Historical Review* 92:3 (June 1987).

Easterby, J.H. ed. *The South Carolina Rice Plantation as Revealed in the Papers of Robert F.W Allston.* Chicago: University of Chicago Press, 1945. Includes chapter on slave and freedom records.

Freedmen's Savings and Trust Deposit Ledger Indexes. Microfilm.

Freedmen's Savings and Trust Signature Books. Microfilm.

Johnson, Michael P. and James L. Roark. *Black Masters: A Free Family of Color in the Old South.* New York: W.W. Norton, 1984. A study of the Ellison family of Charleston.

Koger, Larry. *Free Black Slave Masters in South Carolina 1790-1860.* Jefferson, N.C: McFarland, 1985.

McCuen, Anne K. *Abstracts of Some Greenville County, South Carolina, Records Concerning Black People, Free and Slave.* Spartansburg, S.C: Reprint Co., 1991.

"Records Kept by Colonel Isaac Hayne." *South Carolina and Historical and Genealogical Magazine* 12:1 (January 1911). This installment in a series of Hayne's records contains vital records of slaves 1700-1781.

South Carolina Archives. *State Free Negro Capitation Tax Books Charleston South Carolina circa 1811-1860.* Microfilm. See also the guide to the microfilm publication by Judith M. Brimelow.

South Carolina Historical Society. The Society has reproduced on microfilm a number of Low County church records. Slave baptism records, some quite detailed, are found in many of them. The following show particular promise:
• Calvary Episcopal, Charleston (1848-1978)
• Christ Episcopal, Mount Pleasant , Charleston County (1645-1865)
• Georgetown Methodist Church (1811-1897)
• Holy Communion Episcopal, Charleston (1849-1913)
• Saint Andrew's, Episcopal, Charleston (1719-1783)
• Saint Andrew's, Charleston County (1714-1899)
• Saint Bartholomew's, Colleton County (1818-1861). See in particular "Rector's Journal"
• Saint Helena's, Episcopal, Beaufort County (1720-1830)
• Saint Michael's , Charleston (1751-1981). See in particular "Trapier Register"
• Saint Peter's, Charleston (1834-1958)
• Saint Philip's , Charleston (1713-1984)
• Saint Stephen's , Charleston (1822-1880)
• Sheldon Church, McPhersonville , Hampton County (1825-1932).

Williams, Minnie Simons. *A Colloquial History of a Black South Carolina Family Named Simons.* [Washington, D.C.]: M.S. Williams, 1990.

Wood, Virginia Steele. "Slaves at Rusticello Plantation, Pendleton, Anderson County, South Carolina: Births, Baptisms, Illnesses, Vaccinations, and Deaths." *JAAHGS* 11:3 (fall 1990).

Tennessee

Bamman, Gale Williams. "African Americans Impressed for Service on the Nashville and North Western Railroad, October 1863." *National Genealogical Society Quarterly* 80:3 (September 1992).

Bureau of Refugees, Freedmen and Abandoned Lands. Records of the Assistant Commissioner for Tennessee. Microfilm.

Craighead, Sandra G. "Abstracts from *The Colored Tennessean* 1864-1867: Want Ads for Lost Relations." *JAAHGS* 12:3/4 (fall/winter, 1991).

Freedmen's Savings and Trust Deposit Ledger Indexes. Microfilm.

Freedmen's Savings and Trust Signature Books. Microfilm.

Hamilton, Green Polonius. *The Bright Side of Memphis: A Compendium of Information Concerning the Colored People of Memphis, Tennessee...* Memphis: Burke's Book Store, (1987). Reprint of 1908 edition.

Marsh, Helen C. and Timothy Marsh (editors). *1850 Mortality Schedules.* Shelbyville, Tenn.: Marsh, 1982.

Memphis Riots and Massacres. House of Representatives Report No. 101 (39th Congress, 1st Session). Special Congressional report on the anti-black riots which took place in Memphis in May 1866. Includes extensive testimony and affidavits of many Memphis African Americans, revealing details concerning not only the riots but also information on their families and personal lives. Indexing for witnesses and affiants.

Sistler, Byron and Barbara Sistler. *Tennessee Mortality Schedules.* Nashville: Sistler, 1984. A master index to the 1850, 1860, and 1880 schedules.

Texas

Bureau of Refugees, Freedmen and Abandoned Lands. Records of the Assistant Commissioner for Texas. Microfilm.

A Collection of Pages from the Histories of Neylandville and St. Paul school. Neylandville, Tex.: City of Neylandville, 1988. Neylandville, Hunt County is a predominantly African American community.

Crouch, Barry A. and Larry Madras. *Reconstructing Black Families: Perspectives from the Texas Freedmen's Bureau Records in Our Family, Our Town: Essays on Family and Local History Sources in the National Archives.* Washington, D.C.: National Archives, 1987.

Jones, Howard. *The Red Diary: A Chronological History of Black Americans in Houston and some Neighboring Harris County Communities – 122 Years Later.* Austin, Tex.: Nortex, 1991.

Murray, Joyce Martin. *Austin County, Texas Deed Abstracts: 1837-1852.* Dallas: Murray, 1987. Does not contain as much slave data as does her Red River County volume (see below); however, this book does deserve mention since it, like the Red River volume, contains a slave name index.

_____, *Red River County, Texas Deed Abstracts: Republic of Texas and State of Coahuila and Texas (Mexico).* Dallas: Murray, 1986. Extensive slave index.

Pemberton, Doris Hollis. *Juneteenth at Comanche Crossing.* Austin, Tex.: Eakin, 1983. History of African Americans in Limestone County.

Smith, Gloria L. See entry for this author under North Carolina.

Virginia and West Virginia

Bell, John C. Louisa *County Records You Probably Never Saw.* Nashville, Tenn.: Bell, 1983. Includes free black register 1816-1837.

Bell, Mary McCampbell. "Campbell County, Virginia Manumissions from Deed Books 1-2." *JAAHGS* 7:1 (spring 1986).

Boyd-Rush, Dorothy A. *Register of Free Blacks, Rockingham County, Virginia, 1807-1859.* Bowie, Md.: Heritage, 1992.

Breen, T.H. and Stephen Innes. *Myne Own Ground: Race and Freedom on Virginia's Eastern Shore, 1640-1676.* New York: Oxford University Press, 1980. Scholarly monograph examining free blacks in seventeenth century Northampton County.

Bushman, Katherine G. *Registers of Free Blacks 1810-1864 Augusta County, Virginia and Staunton, Virginia.* Verona, Va.: Mid-Valley Press, 1989.

Records of the Assistant Commissioner for Virginia. Microfilm. See also Gentry (below).

Cerny, Johni. "From Maria to Bill Cosby. A Case Study in Tracing Black Slave Ancestry." *National Genealogical Society Quarterly* 75:1 (March 1987).

Dickinson, Richard B. *Entitled! Free Papers in Appalachia Concerning Antebellum Freeborn Negroes and Emancipated Blacks in Montgomery County, Virginia.* Washington D.C.: National Geographical Society, 1981.

Engs, Robert Francis. *Freedom's First Generation: Black Hampton, Virginia 1861-1890.* Philadelphia: Univ. of Pennsylvania, 1979.

Fitzgerald, Ruth Coder. *A Different Story: A Black History of Fredericksburg, Stafford and Spotsylvania, Virginia.* [s.l.]: Unicorn, 1976.

Flowers, J. Clayton. "Richard Clayton of Surry County Virginia and his Descendants." *JAAHGS* 6:4 (winter 1985).

Freedmen's Savings and Trust Deposit Ledger Indexes. Microfilm.

Frost, Olivia Pleasants. "The Journey of Five Generations of a Freedman's Family." *JAAHGS* 3:2 (summer 1982).

Gentry, Hollis. "Index of Prominent Freedmen in Virginia." *JAAHGS* 10:4 (winter 1989). Refers to the records of the Assistant Commissioner for Virginia of the Bureau of Refugees, Freedmen and Abandoned Lands.

Headley, Robert K. *Genealogical Abstracts from 18th Century Virginia Newspapers.* Baltimore: Genealogical Publishing Co., 1987. Contains numerous references to runaway slaves and free blacks.

Hodge, Robert A. *Birth Records, Fredericksburg, Virginia A-Z (Colored) 1900-1940.* Fredericksburg, Va.: Hodge, 1988.

Some Pre-1871 Vital Statistics on Colored Persons of Culpeper County, Virginia. Fredericksburg, Va.: Hodge, 1978.

Hollie, Donna Tyler. "Blacknell Family Slaves." *JAAHGS* 6:1 (spring 1985).

Johnson, David A.G. (Jr.). "The Coy Family of Virginia: A Documentary Portrait." *JAAHGS* 12:3/4 (fall/winter 1991).

Latimer, Frances Bibbins. *The Register of Free Negroes: Northampton County, Virginia, 1853 to 1861.* Bowie, Md: Heritage, 1992.

"List of Free Blacks in Westmoreland County, Virginia 1801." *The Virginia Genealogist* 31:1 (January-March, 1987).

Lucas, Townsend M. "Loudoun County, Virginia, Documentation on Free Blacks." *JAAHGS* 11:3 (fall 1990).

Madden, T.O. (Jr.) and Ann L. Miller. *We Were Always Free: The Maddens of Culpeper County, Virginia; A 200-Year Family History.* New York: Norton, 1992.

Norris, Mary Boldridge. *Property Tax List of Culpeper, Virginia and Names of Slaves 1783*. Raleigh, N.C.: Norris, 1936.

The Parish Register of Christ Church, Middlesex County, Va. From 1653-1812. Easley, S.C.: Southern Historical Press, 1988. Reprint of 1897 edition. Notable for extensive slave birth and baptism listings.

Pinkard, Ophelia Taylor. "A Record of Slave Membership in Fairfields Baptist Church, Burgess, Northumberland County, Virginia from 1844 to 1864." *JAAHGS* 11:4 (winter 1990).

Taylors of Northumberland County, Virginia. Washington, D.C.: Pinkard, 1987.

Provine, Dorothy S. *Alexandria County, Virginia Free Negro Registers 1797-1861*. Bowie, Md.: Heritage, 1990.

Ragsdale, Willie. "A List of Free Negroes and Mulattos Registered in the County of Lunenberg, Virginia, from 1815 to 1850. *JAAHGS* 11:1&2 (summer & spring 1990).

Ruffin, C. Bernard. "In Search of the Unappreciated Past: The Ruffin-Cornick Family of Virginia." *National Genealogical Society Quarterly* 81:2 (June 1993).

Schreiner-Yantis, Nettie. *The 1787 Census of Virginia*. Springfield, Va.: Genealogical Books in Print 1987. Slaves listed by name in Mecklenburg and Surry Counties, also Nelson County, Kentucky. Free blacks are often identified as such. There is a separate index for free blacks and slaves.

Scott, Jean S. "Charles City County, Virginia, Personal Property Tax." *JAAHGS* 3:3 (fall 1982). Names of Slaves listed with owners in 1784.

"Index to Free Negro Register 1791-1841, Book I, Arlington, Virginia." *JAAHGS* 3:1 (spring 1982).

"Slave Manifest 1833." See District of Columbia heading.

Smith, Gloria L. *Black Americans at Mount Vernon: Genealogy Techniques for Slave Group Research.* Tuscan, Arizona: Smith, 1984.

Slave Documentation: Slaves of Arlington. Tucson, Arizona: Trailstone, 1990. Photos and names of slaves at Robert E. Lee's mansion home.

Solemn Ceremonies: Index of Civil War Marriages, Virginia. Marriage Records of African American Families of Gloucester County, Virginia Area from Record Group 105, Received at Camp Hamilton, Virginia. Tucson, Va.: Smith, 1990.

Stevens, Cj. "Black Births and Baptisms in Mannikintown." *JAAHGS* 4:1 (spring 1983). Primarily slaves of Huguenots in early and mid-eighteenth century Goochland County.

Sweig, Donald. *Registrations of Free Negroes Commencing September Court 1822…* Fairfax, Va.: Fairfax County History Commission, 1977. Fairfax County records.

Thackery, David T. "Crossing the Divide: A Census Study of Slaves before and after Freedom." *Origins* (The Newberry Library) V:2 (March 1989). A study of Hampshire County, West Virginia.

White, Charles W. *The Hidden and Forgotten: Contributions of Buckingham Blacks to American History.* Buckingham, Va.: White, 1985.

Wingo, Elizabeth B. and W. Bruce Wingo. *Norfolk County, Virginia Tithables 1730-1750.* Norfolk, Va.: Wingo, 1979. Also: *Norfolk County, Virginia Tithables 1751-1765.* Norfolk, Va.: Wingo, 1981. Both items especially notable for the fact that slaves are listed with owners.

Wynne, Frances Holloway. *Register of Free Negroes and Also of Dower Slaves, Brunswick County, Virginia 1803-1850.* Fairfax, Va.: Wynne, 1983.

Wisconsin

Cooper, Zachary. *Black Settlers in Rural Wisconsin*. Madison: State Historical Society of Wisconsin, 1977. Focuses on Vernon and Grant Counties.

Addendum: Canada

French, Gary E. *Men of Colour: An Historical Account of the Black Settlement on Wilberforce Street and in Oro Township, Simcoe County, Ontario, 1819-1949*. [Toronto?]: Kaste Books, 1978.

INTERNET SOURCES

Following is a selection of Web sites that contain African American information. While there are many African American sites on the Internet, this list focuses on the major sites that are of obvious genealogical and historical value to researchers of African American ancestors.

AfriGeneas

http://www.afrigeneas.com

With the objective of "providing leadership, promotion and advocacy for the mutual development of genealogy resources for researching African related ancestry," this could be considered one of the most comprehensive African American genealogy sites. An ideal primary destination for any African American researcher, the site is especially helpful for beginners. The sublinks of this site provide more information than most other entire sites.

Of special note is the comprehensive list of related links <http://www.afrigeneas.com/links.html>, as well as the guide to research <http://www.afrigeneas.com/guide/> written by Dee Parmer Woodtor, author of *Finding a Place Called Home: An African-American Guide to Genealogy and Historical Identity* (Random House, 1999).

African American Genealogical Society of Northern California

http://www.aagsnc.org

The Society's stated objective is "to enlighten and enrich self-worth and self-esteem of African Americans through genealogical research and interest, to promote interest in genealogy, biography, and related history among African Americans, to supplement and enrich the education of African Americans through the collection, preservation and maintenance of African American genealogical materials, to promote the accumulation and preservation of African American genealogical and related historical material and make such material available to all, and to promote and maintain ethical standards in genealogical research and publications. This site is a great starting point, with links to many other Internet resources for tracing African American lineage.

African American Lifelines

http://pages.prodigy.net/cliffmurr/aa_life.htm

This site includes beginning steps, and other resources for someone new to researching African American roots. The site includes sections on where to begin, basic research, military records, getting professional research help, spelling conflicts, Freedmen's Bureau, court records, among other topics.

Christine's Genealogy Web site

http://www.ccharity.com

An extensive repository of African American information and records donated by volunteers. Of particular interest to researchers is the site's list of newspaper and magazine articles on African American family history topics. <http://www.ccharity.com/genlinks/Articles/>.

Cyndi's List–African American

http://www.cyndislist.com/african.htm

Cyndi's list has traditionally been known as the end-all for link sites. As could be expected, this compilation of African American-specific sites and resources is top-notch.

The African-American Genealogy Ring

http://www.webring.org/cgi-bin/webring?ring = afamgenring&list

This site has ninety-two listings of African American-related Web sites. Site topics range from the Freedman's Savings & Trust Company to Notable African American Women Ancestors to individual family sites with downloadable GEDCOM files.

Distant Cousin

http://www.distantcousin.com/Links/Ethnic/African/index.html

This African American section of the Distant Cousin Web site contains many useful resources and links.

American Slave Narratives: An Online Anthology
http://xroads.virginia.edu/ ~ HYPER/wpa/wpahome.html
From 1936 to 1938, more than 2,300 former slaves from across the South were interviewed by writers and journalists working for the Works Progress Administration. This Web site provides samples of these narratives, as well as some of the photographs taken at the time of the interviews. Of special note is one narrative that includes audio excerpts from the actual interview.

Montgomery County Public School System
http://www.mcps.k12.md.us/curriculum/socialstd/African_Am_bo okmarks.html
An extensive list of African American history resources from the Montgomery County Public School system in Rockville, Maryland. The sites referenced on this site can add valuable context to any African American research project.

The Lest We Forget Genealogy Page
http://www.coax.net/people/lwf/genes.htm
A list of links, many of which may not be found elsewhere, including many military records.

Prologue (Summer 1997)
http://www.nara.gov/publications/prologue/aframpro.html
This issue of *Prologue* (Summer 1997) "focuses on the use of federal records in African American historical research." It includes sixteen articles by NARA staff and other historians explore the depth and breadth of material in the National Archives relative to African Americans. The issue examines the Civil War and Reconstruction, labor issues, civil rights, pictorial records, and research aids.

Encyclopaedia Brittanica
http://blackhistory.eb.com
This very visual and informative guide to black history includes a comprehensive timeline, study guide, and related links.

Mailing List

http://ftp.cac.psu.edu/ ~ saw/aagene-faq.html

AAGENE-L is intended to be a mailing list on the internet for African American genealogy researchers. "It is also appropriate to discuss African American history within the mailing list."

Mailing List

http://members.aol.com/memery/faq/

According to the site, "The purpose of soc.genealogy.african is to provide a forum for people to share queries and insights regarding the genealogical considerations of Africa and the African Diaspora. The newsgroup is one of a set of related newsgroups that form the soc.genealogy hierarchy. Details of each of these other newsgroups are posted each month in soc.genealogy.computing and other newsgroups."

RESEARCH ADDRESSES

The following African American research addresses were excerpted from The Ancestry Family Historian's Address Book, *published by Ancestry.com.*

African-American Cultural & Genealogical Society

314 North Main Street
P.O. Box 25251
Decatur, IL 62525
Tel: 217-429-7458
URL: http://www.decaturnet.org/afrigenes.html

African-American Genealogy Group (AAGG)

P.O. Box 1798
Philadelphia, PA 19105-1798
Tel: 215-572-6063
Fax: 215-885-7244
URL: http://www.libertynet.org/~gencap/aagg.html

Afro American Historical & Cultural Museum

7th and Arch Streets
Philadelphia, PA 19106
Tel: 215-574-0380
URL: http://www.fieldtrip.com/pa/55740380.htm

Afro-American Historical and Genealogical Society

P.O. Box 73086
Washington, DC 20056
http://www.rootsweb.com/~mdaahgs/

Association for the Study of Afro-American Life and History
7961 Eastern Ave. Ste. 301
Silver Spring, MD 20910
Tel: (301) 5875900

About the Author

Noted genealogist David Thackery passed away on 17 July 1998 at the age of 45 after suffering a heart attack while jogging near his home in Hyde Park, Illinois.

A native of Urbana, Ohio, David had a life-long passion for history and research. He earned a bachelor's degree from Wittenberg University in Springfield, Ohio and two master's degrees from the University of Chicago in library science and divinity. He joined the Newberry in 1982, and was made head of the research facility's local and family history department in 1983.

As head of the department, David dramatically expanded the library's services and collections in the area of family history. In 1988 and 1989, he used a $62,000 grant to buy microfilm from the National Archives to enhance the library's collection of African American family history sources. In his position as curator of local and family history at Chicago's Newberry Library, David spent his last years developing one of the nation's foremost genealogy collections.

David was a prolific writer and bibliographer, contributing articles to major genealogical publications and compiling some of the best bibliographic sources available for African American researchers.